D1761299

ArtScroll Series®

Rabbi Nosson Scherman / Rabbi Meir Zlotowitz

General Editors

Partners in

Published by
Mesorah Publications, ltd

DR. MEIR WIKLER

Parenting

The questions parents ask.
The answers they need.

FIRST EDITION
First Impression … February 2011

Published and Distributed by
MESORAH PUBLICATIONS, LTD.
4401 Second Avenue / Brooklyn, N.Y 11232

Distributed in Europe by
LEHMANNS
Unit E, Viking Business Park
Rolling Mill Road
Jarow, Tyne & Wear, NE32 3DP
England

Distributed in Israel by
SIFRIATI / A. GITLER — BOOKS
6 Hayarkon Street
Bnei Brak 51127

Distributed in Australia and New Zealand
by **GOLDS WORLDS OF JUDAICA**
3-13 William Street
Balaclava, Melbourne 3183
Victoria, Australia

Distributed in South Africa by
KOLLEL BOOKSHOP
Ivy Common
105 William Road
Norwood 2192, Johannesburg, South Africa

ARTSCROLL SERIES®
PARTNERS IN PARENTING
© Copyright 2011, by MESORAH PUBLICATIONS, Ltd.
4401 Second Avenue / Brooklyn, N.Y. 11232 / (718) 921-9000 / www.artscroll.com

ISBN 10: 1-4226-1089-6 / ISBN 13: 978-1-4226-1089-3

Typography by CompuScribe at ArtScroll Studios, Ltd.

Bound by Sefercraft, Quality Bookbinders, Ltd., Brooklyn N.Y. 11232

*T*his book is dedicated in loving tribute to
my dear brother-in-law and sister-in-law,

Rabbi Yisroel Meir and Feige Ferber עמו״ש

*W*hose exceptional children each reflect
the sterling middos, ahavas chesed,
and deep-rooted emunah
instilled in them by their parents.
Mindful of Rashi's comment (Shemos 6:23)
and the words of Chazal (Bava Basra 110a),
"Most children turn out like their mother's brother,"
I have always felt uniquely honored to have
Srully for a brother-in-law.
His hasmadah is enviable;
his outstanding reputation for honesty is well deserved;
and his cheerful disposition is his trademark.

May Hashem Yisbarach grant
Srully and Feige
continued good health and
much Yiddishe nachas,
עד מאה ועשרים שנה.

Rabbi CHAIM P. SCHEINBERG
Rosh Hayeshiva "TORAH ORE"
and Morah Hora'ah of Kiryat Mattersdorf

הרב חיים פינחס שיינברג
ראש ישיבת "תורה אור"
ומורה הוראה דקרית מטרסדורף

בס"ד
אלול תש"ע

מכתב ברכה

The mitzvah of חינוך בנים is one that stands עולם של עולם. And ברומו של עולם. And we mention it twice a day, as it is included in the words of קריאת שמע: "ושננתם לבניך" (דברים ו:ז). On those words, the Ramban writes, "Behold, we are commanded that our children should know the mitzvos. And how should they know them if we do not teach them?" That is the mitzvah of חינוך בנים.

Today, many parents feel confused and bewildered about how to fulfill the mitzvah of חינוך בנים properly. For that reason, I am happy to see that Dr. Meir Wikler has just completed this, his third volume on the subject, entitled, *Partners in Parenting*. In it, readers will find practical advice in dealing with common challenged which parents face even more now than ever before.

I have known Dr. Wikler for many years and I know him to be a true בן תורה whose יראת שמים has not been compromised by his professionalism. May he see much success from this ספר and from all of his ספרים.

חיים פינחס שיינברג

רחוב פנים מאירות 2, ירושלים, ת.ד. 6979, טל. 1513–537 (02), ישראל
2 Panim Meirot St., Jerusalem, P.O.B. 6979, Tel. (02) 537-1513, Israel

RABBI YAAKOV PERLOW
1569 - 47TH STREET
BROOKLYN N.Y. 11219

יעקב פרלוב
קהל עדת יעקב נאוואמינסק
ישיבת נאוואמינסק - קול יהודא
ברוקלין. נ.י.

בס"ד ‏סיון תשנ"ז

Dr. Meir Wikler has been a wise counselor and therapist for many years. His current book, Partners in Parenting, results from his vast experience in dealing with family problems in our community, a book which, I'm sure, will be a most useful guide for the many parents seeking help and advice in the raising of children. Dr. Wikler's approach coincides with the Torah values he possesses, and I hope his new book will be a helpful resource in bringing out the finest in the young generation growing up in our midst.

With all best wishes

R. Yaakov Perlow

Rabbi Abraham J. Twerski, M.D.

17 Cheshvan, 5771
October 25, '10

One may not drive an automobile unless one has proven one has the competence to do so properly. Just the fact that one's parents drove a car does not authorize one to do so. Yet, the single most awesome function a person has, parenting a child, is generally executed as if one was naturally endowed with competence in parenting. Is it any wonder that our youth is problem-ridden, and that they carry these problems into adult life, passing them on to their children?

Young people would be wise to prepare themselves to be parents. *Partners in Parenting* by Dr. Meir Wikler is an excellent source of guidance for parents and parents-to-be. Dr. Wikler brings decades of counseling experience to this most vital of all human responsibilities. The multi-generational mistakes in parenting must be reversed. Partners in Parenting is a must reading.

Rabbi Abraham J. Twerski, M.D.

Rabbi Paysach J. Krohn

117-09 85th Avenue • Kew Gardens, NY 11418
(718) 846-6900 • Fax (718) 846-6903
e-mail: krohnmohel@brisquest.com • www.brisquest.com

January 2011/Shvat 5771

Dear Reader;

You are about to travel on a journey through life with a delightful, perceptive individual who will teach you, with wisdom and humor, how to handle your family's trickiest and most sensitive moments. Infants, adolescents, teenagers and married children each provide their own set of trials, tribulations, doubts and dilemmas that parents must deal with.

A simple conflict can turn into a conflagration of resentment if not handled properly. Tragically many families have been ripped asunder by a lack of understanding of what is right, what is expected, and what can be tolerated. Dr. Meir Wikler is well equipped to guide parents with both short term and long term solutions to a family crisis. He is a noted lecturer, a highly regarded psychotherapist, a prolific writer, a marriage therapist, and an 'ehrlicher Yid' who is worth listening to.

One of my favorite insights from Dr. Wikler is a bit of advice he gave at a conference on Sholom Bayis. He said, "The three most important words in marriage are ….not the ones you are thinking about, rather 'I was wrong!'" Admitting a wrong goes a long way in patching and rebuilding a relationship.

I once used this teaching in a lecture and afterwards I heard a man go over to his wife and say, "Did you hear what the rabbi said? You are wrong!" That fellow surely did not learn the lesson. He missed the point completely.

Dear reader, if you do not take the time to read this book, I will have no choice but to point to you and say, "You are wrong!" It is worth your time and effort to study the timeless answers given to the questions that hundreds of parents have posed. I am honored to be considered Dr. Wikler's friend and after you read his words you will feel that you are his friend as well. He is warm, kind and convincing. Enjoy the book.

Respectfully,

Paysach J. Krohn

Table of Contents

1. *Infants and Preschool-Age Children*

2. *Elementary School-Age Children*

3. Teenagers

4. *Young Adults and Beyond*

Acknowledgments

I welcome this opportunity to publicly proclaim my heartfelt gratitude to *Hashem Yisbarach* for the *siyata di'Shmaya* which enabled me to complete this third book on *chinuch habanim*. "*Mah ashiv la'Hashem kol tagmulohi alai* (How can I repay *Hashem* for all He has bestowed upon me?)" (*Tehillim* 116:12).

In addition, I would like to acknowledge those people who contributed in any way to this book and without whom its publication would not have been possible.

First and foremost, I would like to thank all of the children, adolescents and their parents with whom I have been privileged to work, who taught me more about the realities and dynamics of family life than I ever could have learned in a classroom or from textbooks. As David HaMelech said, "*Mikol m'lamdai his'kalti*, I became wise from all of those whom I have taught" (*Tehillim* 119:99).

I would also like to thank all those parents who took the time to send their parenting questions to me via *Hamodia* so that I could answer them in my column, which served as the forerunner to this book.

I am also grateful to the following individuals:

Grand Rabbi Levi I. Horowitz, the *Bostoner Rebbe, ztz"l,* for his lifelong inspiration, guiding hand, boundless *chesed,* and intimate concern for me and my family and for his *haskamos* for my first two books on parenting;

Hagaon Harav Chaim P. Scheinberg, *shlita,* for his perennially open door, and for his *haskamah;*

Harav Yaakov Perlow, the *Novominsker Rebbe, shlita,* for his *shiurim,* priceless guidance, longstanding personal interest, and his *haskamah;*

Harav Shlomo Brevda, *shlita,* for his *shiurim,* sage counsel, making my concerns his concerns, and for his *haskamah;*

Rabbi Dr. Abraham Twerski, for his profound inspiration, personal friendship, and for his *haskamah;*

Rabbi Paysach Krohn, for his enduring friendship, his enthusiastic support and encouragement, and for his *haskamah;*

Rabbi Yaakov Salomon, L.C.S.W., a *yedid ne'eman*, for his creative contributions to this book and all aspects of my professional life, and for his uncompromising personal commitment to me, in times of both joy and challenge;

Dr. Gail Bessler, Dr. Larry Bryskin, Dr. Rashi Shapiro, Dr. Bentzion Sorotzkin, and Dr. Elin Weinstein, the current members of the professional peer-supervision group to which I have belonged for the past 27 years, for providing me a fertile forum in which to cultivate many of the concepts, insights, and formulations included here and for their encouragement to compile and complete this book;

Rabbi Meir Zlotowitz and Rabbi Nosson Scherman, General Editors of ArtScroll/Mesorah Publications, for their vote of confidence by including me in the ArtScroll "family"; and to the following dedicated Artscroll staff: Mrs. Judi Dick, for her expert editing of the manuscript, her invaluable suggestions, and, most of all, for the high regard and dedication she showed this project from the outset; Mr. Avrohom Biderman and Mr. Mendy Herzberg for their faithful shepherding of the manuscript through all stages of publication; Mr. Eli Kroen, for his masterful design of the cover. I would also like to express my appreciation to Mrs. Faygie Weinbaum for her meticulous proofreading; Mrs. Sury Englard for the exquisite layout which greatly enhances the book, and for the final corrections; Mrs. Esther Feierstein and Mrs. Toby Goldzweig for entering the additions or corrections. Their input was invaluable.

Sarah, Yeshaya, Miriam Baila, Shloimy, Dovi, and Rivky for always giving me so much *nachas*;

"*Achronah, achronah, chavivah,*" my wife, Malka, for her faithful support and patient indulgence throughout my career for which she deserves all of the credit for whatever I have accomplished, with the help of *Hashem*. Of her it may be said, "That which is mine and that which is yours — all belongs to her" (*Kesubos* 63a).

Preface

As all parents understand, raising children is very much a partnership enterprise. *Chazal*, for example, have taught, "There are three partners in [the creation of] man: *Hakadosh Baruch Hu*, his father, and his mother" (*Kiddushin* 30b).

Moreover, in today's complex, high-pressured, and high-powered world filled with high anxiety, parents often have to reach out and engage additional partners to help them raise their children. Besides *mechanchim* and teachers, parents sometimes enlist the expertise of pediatricians, tutors, speech therapists, psychologists, and social workers. They also turn to their own parents, other relatives, and friends for advice. And, of course, they should always seek guidance from their *rebbe'im, roshei hayeshivah* and *rabbanim.*

In addition to these partners, parents also seek out the expertise of those who share their parenting wisdom and experience through books and recorded lectures. And, as if all of that were not enough, parents also avail themselves of insights and recommendations found in parenting advice columns published by almost every periodical catering to the Torah community.

Since July, '09, I have had the privilege of writing a weekly column, "Partners in Parenting," for the daily *Hamodia*. Many of these columns were also reprinted in the international, weekly edition of that paper. Through the medium of that column, I have been consulted by hundreds of parents who have submitted their questions on a wide range of parenting concerns. And through my published responses, I have become a partner with them, as well as with the countless others who read the column; hence, the title of this book.

Most of the chapters of this book, therefore, originally appeared in my weekly *Hamodia* column and they are reprinted here with the permission of the publisher. All of them have been edited, and in most cases expanded, for this book, thereby including considerable material that did not appear in the original columns. Although the chapters are organized into four chronological categories, each chapter contains insights and practical advice that would be useful to parents of children of any age.

Chazal have stated, "*Shiv'im panim laTorah*, There are seventy faces to the Torah" (*Bamidbar Rabbah* 13:15). And although the different opinions may, at times, even contradict one another, like the views of Hillel and Shamai, "*Eilu v'eilu, divrei Elokim chayim*, these and those are both the words of the living G-d" (*Eruvin* 13b, *Gittin* 6b).

Just as this is so in interpreting the *Torah shebich'sav*, the written Torah, so too does this apply to the *Toras habayis*, the Torah guidelines for family relations. When it comes to parenting, therefore, there is simply no one right way to do things. Children can grow up in homes that are run very, very differently and still become satisfied, secure, and successful adults.

If there is no single, proper approach to parenting, then why write a book on the subject?

While there may not be a *single* correct method of raising children, there are some techniques which have been proven to be much more successful than others.

This book was not designed, therefore, to be used as the final word on any of the subjects covered. Rather, it was conceived to provide some insights into childhood and adolescent behavior, offer some practical suggestions and a list of options for meeting the daily challenges of *chinuch habanim* (parenthood) and stimulate some thought and discussion about matters which should concern every Jewish parent, today.

It is not my goal to have readers angrily confront their spouses, jabbing the print on these pages with their forefingers and declaring, "See, even Dr. Wikler says that parents should. . .!" What would gratify me, however, would be for readers to put this book down (gently) and turn to their spouses, remarking, "You know, the chapter I just read has caused me to stop and think. Maybe we need to reevaluate the way we've been handling the situation at home with our children."

This book is intended for recently married couples standing on the threshold of parenthood as they look forward to the birth of their first child; young parents with small children who are groping to "get a handle" on what parenthood is all about; parents of school-age children who are searching for fresh strategies to use in dealing with recurrent child rearing dilemmas; parents of adolescents who are finding new meaning in the phrase, "end of my rope"; and, finally, child, adolescent, and family thera-pists who are seeking to enhance their clinical skills by comparing notes with a colleague.

Parenting can be a lonely, thankless, and frustrating proposition. But it can also be rewarding, uplifting, and deeply gratifying. It is my fervent wish that this book help parents avoid the former experience and achieve the latter.

Ideally, this will not be a book which is read once and then used to steady wobbly furniture. Rather, it is my hope that through this book, I may serve as a constant, supportive, and encouraging partner to parents as they traverse the winding, sometimes thorny, but always noble, path of parenthood.

Meir Wikler, D.S.W.
Brooklyn, New York

1 Infants and Preschool-Age Children

My 5-Year-Old Son Became Hysterical When His Goldfish Died

One of the advantages of living in our neighborhood is the abundance of back-yard carnivals that take place during the warmer weather. These impromptu festivities provide entrepreneur training and extra spending money for the older organizers, entertainment and excitement for the younger customers, and a much-needed break for the mothers of all the children involved.

My 5-year-old son recently attended one of these local carnivals and came home proudly toting a live goldfish. As his two older sisters are both rather squeamish about live creatures of any kind, this poor fellow was the first pet to have taken up residence in our home.

We certainly do not own the proper equipment nor do I possess the necessary experience to adequately care for this new addition to our family. So, unfortunately, the fish died two days later.

I knew my son would be upset about this so I disposed of it before he came home from school. In fact, I'm not really sure what I was thinking at the time. Perhaps I was hoping that he would not notice the fish's absence. Boy, was I mistaken! As soon as he walked in the door, he insisted on knowing what happened to his fish.

Not wanting to lie, I told him that it died. Then he demanded to know where it was. When I told him that I had to flush it, he became hysterical. He simply could not be calmed down. He was furious and pressured me to buy him another one. I was tempted to do so but I knew the next fish would certainly meet the same fate.

Considering the upheaval this caused, I suspect that I may have mishandled this episode. Should I have kept the dead fish? Should I have agreed to buy him a new one? Please advise me.

Let's begin with what you did right. You did not lie. If you are a regular reader of my column, you should know by now that lying to children is never the thing to do.

Your mistake, however, was trying to shield your son from his loss. You knew he would be upset and he was. But grief and sadness are not uncommon, unnatural feelings. On the contrary, they are a normal part of daily life.

Shlomo HaMelech declared, "There is a time for crying and a time for laughter; a time to eulogize and a time to dance" (*Koheles* 3:4). In other words, all feelings have their appropriate time and place.

The job of a parent is not to shield his or her children from all pain, discomfort, and unpleasantness. Rather, it is the responsibility of parents to teach their children how to deal properly with all of life's circumstances.

Take germs for example. Parents who expose their children to illness or unsanitary conditions are guilty of neglect and can be prosecuted for that. But parents who attempt to quarantine their children in a compulsively sanitized environment are not helping them either. Every pediatrician will tell you that children need to ingest *some* germs in order to build up sufficient antibodies in their systems to ward of more serious illnesses when they get older.

Similarly, children need to be allowed to experience all of the emotions inherent in daily living so that they will learn how to deal with the full range of their human feelings.

At 5 years old, your son may be too young to deal with the intense grief displayed at a *levayah*. But he was not too young to have witnessed his prized goldfish floating lifelessly in the bowl in your home. Then you would have had the opportunity to discuss his feelings without your having violated his "property rights" complicating the discussion.

After answering his questions and talking about his feelings, you could have then discussed the question of how to dispose of the deceased fish. Including your son in the decision-making process would have empowered him and respected his feelings. I am not suggesting here that you should have given your son complete control. Had he refused to allow you to discard the fish, for example, that wish could obviously not be honored.

Writing these lines now I am recalling the death of my first pet, a minnow I had scooped up one summer in my sand pail when I was not yet 4 years old. And I can still remember the feelings of grief that washed over me when I discovered it floating belly up in the pail the next morning.

My mother, *a"h*, explained to me that we could not keep it because it would smell up the entire bungalow. She gently informed me that we would have to send it away in one way or another. But she asked me to think about my preference.

I asked if we could return it to the water from where I had scooped it up the day before. As it was not far from our bungalow, my mother acquiesced to my request. And the fact that I can recall this incident today, so many years later, attests to the impact it had on me and the sensitive manner in which my mother handled it.

Parents have an awesome responsibility to guide, educate, and train their children. In addition to all of the many subjects covered by that mandate that we take for granted, teaching children how to manage their feelings is one topic that is too often overlooked. And one of the reasons it is neglected is because many parents are clueless as to how to go about it.

So what can parents do if they want to help their children learn how to cope with the full range of emotions but they do not know how? Aside from reading this book, parents can purchase a copy of *Stories Straight From Avi's Heart* by Raanan and Walder (Feldheim, 2004).

In addition to sadness, this delightful, beautifully illustrated children's book covers many other feelings such as, disappointment, jealousy, anger, and happiness. Each story focuses on a particular feeling, which is creatively woven into a real life, everyday situation with which any small child can easily identify. As explained quite lucidly in the preface for parents, these stories are meant to be read and then discussed with children.

As has been stated here in the past, the single most valuable thing parents can do for children to maximize their academic success in school is to read them bedtime stories. In addition to providing a warm, intimate bonding opportunity for parents and children, it pumps into a child priceless language skills that have been clinically proven to advance a child's reading ability which practically guarantees higher grades.

A few years from now, when your son is older, you will have another option available for teaching him how to manage his feelings. And that is modeling it for him. Right now, however, he is too young to be able to learn from your example.

By modeling, I am referring to sharing your own coping skills with your children. For example, suppose you found yourself in a very stressful situation recently. What did you do to make yourself feel better? What words of *chizuk* or encouragement did you think to yourself? Disclosing such episodes of firsthand coping with older children is helpful for them.

Sitting at the Shabbos table, it might sound something like this. "While we were in Eretz Yisrael, we took a taxi from the *Kosel*. On the way back to our *dirah*, we got caught in terrible traffic. A ride that should have cost us around 30 *shekels*, cost us over 60! At first, I was so upset, frustrated and angry. But then I remembered that a friend I had met in Eretz Yisrael had just lost her wallet. Compared to that misfortune, I really should be dancing, I thought to myself. Then the exorbitant cost of the taxi didn't bother me as much as before."

Some parents might object to making such self-disclosures. They don't want to let their children know that they respond to life's trials and tribulations with anything less than exemplary deportment. "I'm supposed to set a good example for my kids," they would say. "I don't want them to know that I get angry when I should not have."

What these parents fail to realize is that by sharing their feelings with their children they are also teaching their children how adults process and manage those feelings. The children then learn how to cope with a wide range of natural human emotions. On the other hand, if parents attempt to mask their true feelings and pretend that they never experience loneliness, disappointment, shame or rejection, then their children will be ill equipped to cope with such emotions when they experience them themselves.

Our 3½-Year-Old Takes Other Children's Toys

In your column on "Confronting Theft," you wrote, "in almost all cases of children who stole from family members, the children were acting out their frustration with the distant relationship they had with one or both parents."

Both my husband and I believe that we have an excellent relationship with our son, who is almost 4 years old. We have two other children, a boy, 2, and a girl who is 3 months old.

Both my husband and I spend lots of time with our oldest, who almost always accompanies us on errands and shopping trips. We read him stories and get down on the floor to play games with him, not just because he asks, but because we enjoy doing so ourselves.

Recently, however, we have noticed that he comes home from my in-laws' house with small toys that do not belong to him. My husband is the oldest in his family and he has younger siblings who are contemporaries of our son. So he is often at my in-laws' house playing with his aunts and uncles.

We have tried to explain to our son that he cannot take things that do not belong to him. Just as he would not want any playmate to walk off with any of his toys, he must respect the possessions of other children, as well.

In spite of these "talks," we still find small items in his pockets or at home that do not belong to him. When confronted, he will lie and say his aunt or uncle "gave" him the toy. When we check, however, we find this not to be so.

As far as we can tell, our son is not stealing from friends. Since he is stealing only from family members, we are at a loss to identify the problem in our relationship with him that may be causing him to act out in this way. And we do not know whether and how we should punish him for this misbehavior. Can you offer us any guidance?

Your letter is appreciated for two reasons. Firstly, it is gratifying to know that my columns are being read and taken seriously. And, secondly, it affords me this opportunity to clarify an important issue regarding childhood stealing.

Whenever any childhood behavior is discussed and evaluated, one term which must always be included in that conversation is, "age appropriate." Take pacifier-sucking for example. If an infant is sucking on his or her pacifier during the day, that is normal, age-appropriate behavior. We expect infants to do that. If a 5-year-old is walking around sucking on a pacifier during the day, we would consider that to be age-inappropriate behavior. By 5 years old, therefore, we would expect that a child would either be completely free of his or her pacifier, or, at least use it only at bedtime.

For a 14-year-old to take $200 from his grandfather's safe is clearly age-inappropriate behavior. We would certainly expect a 14-year-old to know better and to realize how wrong that is.

To characterize a 3½-year-old's taking another child's toy as "stealing," however, is somewhat of an overreaction.

Please do not misunderstand. I am not condoning your son's behavior. It is most definitely unacceptable. But you must bear in mind that violating the rights of others is not at all uncommon among preschool-aged children. They simply have not yet developed sufficient internal impulse controls to discipline themselves. The process of socialization takes time. And for many children, at 3½, they still need help in learning how to respect the rights of others.

As the Torah states, "A person's evil impulses begin from his youth" (*Bereishis* 8:21). And on that *pasuk*, Rashi comments, "[The word for youth is] *n'urav*, [which comes to teach us that] from the time when a child begins to move to leave his mother's womb, his *yeitzer hara* is implanted into him." And disrespecting the rights of others is a clear manifestation of the *yeitzer hara*.

You should not be blaming yourselves, therefore, for your son's misbehavior. When older children steal money it often represents a cry for help, acting out their disappointment or frustration with their relationship with either or both parents. When very young children take each other's toys, however, it represents a not-yet-fully-developed level of impulse control.

Even though taking other children's toys may not be uncommon among 3½-year-olds, how should parents respond to such behavior?

The *Gemara* sets out the guideline we all must follow in confronting the *yeitzer hara*. "*Hakadosh Baruch Hu* said to Yisroel, 'My sons, I have created the *yeitzer hara* and I have created the antidote in Torah. And if you will be involved in the study of Torah, you will not be given over into the hands of [the *yeitzer hara*]' " (*Kiddushin* 30b).

What we see from this *Gemara* is that parents must help their children overcome their *yeitzer hara* and improper character traits by teaching them both the study of Torah and the practice of proper *middos* and behavior.

On a more practical level, you should chastise your son each time you discover some toy in his possession that does not belong to him. You should continue to explain to him that just as he would not appreciate having any of his toys pocketed by his playmates so, too, should he respect the possessions of others. In addition, it would be sufficient punishment if you made him return each toy to its owner, under your supervision. That would serve to make him think twice about repeating his behavior in the future.

Finally, you should see this as a learning process which may take several weeks for your son to master. And as with any other teaching endeavor, such as learning the *alef bais*, patience on the part of the instructor is an essential ingredient for a successful outcome.

What Can I Do to Avoid Power Struggles With My 3½-Year-Old Daughter?

My daughter, the oldest of three, is 3½-years old. She is generally a good, friendly girl who is very happy in her *gan* (preschool class). Recently, however, she has become disobedient, turning direct commands, such as, "Go out of the room," or even, "*Please* go out," into power struggles.

When I threaten her with a punishment, such as not getting ice cream for dessert, she replies, "So what? I will take some for myself."

If I take her to her room, she comes right back out.

What can I do not to get into these power struggles? Thank you very much.

Chazal teach that, "A dream that is not interpreted is like a letter that is not read" (*Berachos* 55b). Similarly, a sudden behavioral change in a child is a message to the parents that something may be adversely affecting that child. If the parents ignore the change and simply chalk it up to, "That's the way kids are sometimes," then they may be overlooking an important signal.

You mentioned that your daughter's disobedience is not a chronic problem but only surfaced "recently." In the past, she was much better behaved. We must ask ourselves, therefore, what may have caused this new departure from her formerly friendly disposition?

For example, is she experiencing some stress at school? Is someone starting up with her on the bus? Have there been any personnel changes at school? Is she being bullied or harassed by any of her classmates? Or, is it possible that she is being victimized by someone in the neighborhood?

No, the fact that a child has suddenly become disobedient does not *always* indicate that any of the problems listed above are taking place. But *sometimes* it does. It is always recommended, therefore, that whenever a child displays a sudden change in behavior such questions do need to be asked.

Just from the information you provided, however, we could speculate that your daughter may be struggling with jealous or competitive feelings triggered by sibling rivalry. You did not indicate when her youngest sister was born. Whether it was recently or not, your oldest daughter may be feeling more competition now. And the fact that she is happy in *gan* is not a contradiction. In *gan* she is not confronted by her two younger rivals.

Older children do not always see younger siblings as threats to their position in the family as soon as the younger sibs are born. Older children — especially young ones like your daughter — do not even see infants as people. They are often viewed more as novelties or pets. When the infants begin to babble, sit up, and move around, they are then viewed more as tiny people and, consequently, as more serious threats to their older siblings.

If the full impact of having two younger sisters is only hitting your oldest daughter now, what can you do to help her cope with the new landscape of your family?

The first and most important thing you can do is talk to her about her feelings. Even at $3\frac{1}{2}$, children can verbalize their emotions, albeit in a primitive fashion. The more your daughter can talk about her feelings toward her younger sisters the less likely she will be to act out her frustrations through disobedient behavior.

The second thing you can do is reassure her of her secure and honored position in the family. Give her chores or responsibilities at home whenever possible. And then be sure to praise her lavishly for completing them. "You are Mommy's big helper," "I do not know how I would manage without you around," and "We are so lucky to have you in our family," are refrains you should be singing whenever you can. Some parents believe that children should not be excessively praised for doing what is normally expected of them. They balk, therefore, at any suggestion of lavishly dispensing approval. If these parents need to extricate themselves from power struggles with a disobedient child, however, even they may need to bend their rules in order to achieve compliance with their wishes.

If you make *challah*, for example, let her help. Give her a small piece of dough and let her shape it. Then bake it together with the ones you braided. And be sure to make a fuss over her *challah* at the *Shabbos* table.

Furthermore, point out to her the things you are letting her do because she is "older," "the oldest," or, "the big girl at home." Reinforce in her mind that there are perks for being the oldest so that she will feel proud of her position in the family. In this way, you can minimize — although certainly not eliminate — the deleterious effects of sibling rivalry.

Finally, I must correct you. It is not your daughter who is turning your interactions "into a power struggle." You are the one who is at least partially responsible for the defiance you described.

More specifically, parental guidance and instructions should hardly ever be issued as "commands." Only in an emergency, such as a fire, *chas v'shalom*, should parents command their children to do anything. And make no mistake here. We are not quibbling over the meaning of a single word because the example you gave, "Go out of the room," is undeniably a *command*.

"What is so terrible about commanding children to do things?" you might ask. Your parents commanded you all the time and, boy, did you listen — or else!

Yes, your parents issued commands and you listened. That is why you are repeating the same parenting style with your children. But what worked a generation ago simply does not work today. As Harav Pam, *ztz"l*, often said, "Reproof is most effective when it is given softly and calmly. It rarely works when given with the proverbial, 'fire and brimstone'" (*The Pleasant Way* by Rabbi Shalom Smith, p. 209).

Harav Shlomo Wolbe, *ztz"l*, in his classic *Z'riah U'binyan B'chinuch* (Feldheim, p. 26), quoted Harav Chaim Volozhin, "Nowadays, harsh [words] are not listened to." Harav Wolbe added, "Only soft, pleasant words are listened to . . . [But] what should be done when a child does not listen? You must repeat yourself over and over until the child does listen."

My friend and colleague, Dr. Benzion Sorotzkin, recently shared with me the following passage from Rabbi Gamliel Rabinowitz's *sefer*,

Tiv HaTorah (on *Bereishis*). "[From the way Avraham Avinu spoke to Yitzchak (*Bereishis* 22:7)] we learn that it is important for parents to speak warmly and respectfully to children . . . because in this way they will have a greater influence on them . . . In our generation today, it is only with love and respect that parents can successfully be *mechaneich* their children." Yitzchak called out, "My father." Avraham Avinu replied simply, "Here I am, my son." According to Rabbi Rabinowitz, however, that is an expression reserved for instances when one wishes to display honor to another person.

Regarding the use of punishment, Harav Wolbe (*op. cit.* p.23) emphasized, "Punishment must be the parenting strategy of last resort."

Finally, to talk *tachlis,* so to speak, suppose your daughter is in the room where you are and you need her to leave. What should you do? How should you handle that situation?

If there is any way *you* can leave instead of her, that would make your life a lot easier. Doctors learned a long time ago that the length of patient visits can be drastically reduced if the doctor exits to the next examining room to see another patient rather than wait for the first patient to get up and go.

If that is not an option, then you could present it more in a positive manner, such as, "I really need something from the kitchen now. Could you be my big helper and get it for me? You would make me very happy."

If there is nothing you need or can think of, then you can still word your request pleasantly. For example, "I need to be alone for a few minutes now. If you go out for a few minutes, I'll read you a story when I'm done." If there is no time for the story, however then, at least you can tell your daughter, "It will make me very proud of you if you would do what I am asking now. I know you'd rather not. But I would really appreciate it if you would just step out for a little while. Thank you so much."

At first, you may feel uncomfortable or even awkward to speak to your daughter this way. If you do so, however, the benefits will be self-evident.

Finally, you must bear in mind that threats of punishment are like strong medicine with serious side effects. In emergency situations, they may be worth the risks involved. To use them on a regular basis will only create more problems.

Threats of punishment do sometimes gain compliance. But they come with a heavy cost. The unintended consequences of such a strategy is that they can and often do provoke within the child a desire to rebel and/or test parental limits. And your letter contains an excellent illustration of just that.

Once you threatened your daughter with no dessert, your daughter was provoked to challenge your authority by issuing her own threat to take some for herself. At that point you were faced with the dilemma of a drug addict: take the same amount of drugs and not get high or increase the amount. In other words, in order to gain the compliance you sought you would have had to increase your threat. As you can see, this becomes a slippery slope that produces only losers and no winners. If you back down from a threat, you undermine your own authority; if you escalate the threat level, you provoke your daughter's resentment and rebellion.

Had you praised your daughter for good behavior, however, you would have given her sufficient incentive to avoid misbehavior. And you would have avoided boxing yourself into the no-win situation you described in your letter.

Our 5-Year-Old
Witnessed a Serious Accident

Recently, three of our children witnessed a frightening scene and we are concerned that one of them may have been significantly affected by it.

We have, *bli ayin hara*, nine children, ranging in age from 25 to 3. One afternoon, about four weeks ago, our 17-year-old daughter was outside supervising while her 3- and 5-year-old sisters were playing with a friend. Suddenly, a car, swerving to avoid a cat in the street, jumped the curb and struck my children's 4-year-old playmate. The injured girl was rushed to the hospital by Hatzalah and needed many stitches to close a deep cut in her leg.

Ever since that episode, our 5-year-old has not been herself. Our 3-year-old was also quite shaken that day. The next day, though, she appeared to bounce right back.

Since witnessing the accident, our 5-year-old, however, has been somewhat anxious and high strung. And she seems to overreact now whenever anyone in the family suffers a minor injury. She becomes overly concerned, profusely offers to help, and expresses much more anxiety than would be warranted by the simple cut or bruise the family member has sustained.

We do understand that our daughter is probably still reacting to the frightening scene she witnessed four weeks earlier. But we are now wondering how much longer this will go on and whether or not there is anything we should be doing to help her get over this.

It does sound as if your 5-year-old's change in behavior is a result of her recent trauma. A traumatic event is one in which a person was threatened by or sustained serious injury, or one in which a person witnessed the serious injury of someone else. By definition, the event aroused extreme fear, helplessness, and/or horror. Because young children are more vulnerable than adults and have less well-developed coping skills, they tend to become even more easily traumatized than adults.

When someone has become traumatized, whether an adult or a child, it is not uncommon to experience one or more of the following symptoms: distressing recollections of the event, recurrent nightmares or flashbacks, avoidance of people, places or events associated with the trauma, sleep disturbance, difficulty concentrating, and hypervigilance.

Depending upon the seriousness of the trauma, these symptoms can persist for days, weeks, and even months. So it is not at all unusual for your daughter to still be anxious four weeks after witnessing the accident.

Common sense would dictate that you should ignore the episode, avoid all discussion of it, and your daughter will forget about it and move on. Nothing could be further from the truth. What is needed is what is called, "traumatic-event debriefing."

Firefighters, police, and Hatzalah members are all exposed to traumatic events at some time in the course of their careers. They and their supervisors all know that they must be encouraged to talk about these horrifying events as soon after witnessing them as possible, in order to reduce the long-term impact of the trauma.

As the wisest of all men, Shlomo HaMelech, observed, "A man should always talk out the worry on his heart" (*Mishlei* 12:25; also see the comment on this *pasuk* in *Yoma* 75a that one should, "talk it out to others").

If this strategy is necessary for emergency personnel and first responders to protect themselves from emotional scarring following a traumatic episode, then it is even more critical for children to be debriefed following a trauma.

How should parents go about debriefing a 5-year-old child?

First and foremost, the child should be encouraged to talk about what he or she saw. Even if parents know what happened, they should still ask their child to describe the scene. This report is not needed for the parents to learn any new information. Rather, it is necessary for the child to discharge and vent his or her intense emotions.

The next step is for the parents to ask the child about the child's thoughts and feelings, both during the episode as well as in the immediate aftermath. This is something that adults tend to do automatically after they have been traumatized. Children, however, may only do this if they are encouraged to do so by their parents.

While they are listening to their child vent, parents must avoid any and all moralization and/or judgmentalism. All of the child's thoughts and feelings, therefore, should be accepted and validated. Parents can and should make comments such as, "Of course you were frightened! I would have been frightened, too, if I were there." Or, "Anyone would think that way. That was completely normal for you to think such thoughts."

Finally, the child should be encouraged to raise any questions he or she has about the incident. Children may ask, "Will she die?" "Was it my fault because I said, 'I'm not your friend,' just before it happened?" Or, "How do I know it won't happen to me next time I play outside?" Only after the child has expressed his or her fears should parents offer reassurance. When doing so, parents must be honest and factual, and never make exaggerated, unsubstantiable claims simply to quiet the child's fears. (I.e., "This will never, ever happen again to you or anyone you know.") Such unrealistic claims prove ineffective because children can doubt their veracity. Rather, parents should say something more realistic such as, "I don't ever remember anything like that happening before. So this was a very unusual occurrence. Therefore, it is extremely unlikely that it will happen again, and certainly not to anyone on our block, *chas v'shalom.*"

This process of debriefing is not supposed to take place only during a single conversation on the day of the trauma. In order to be most effective, it needs to be repeated frequently in the aftermath of any trauma.

In case you have not had a debriefing conversation with your daughter, therefore, it is not too late. You can have that conversation with her today and it can still have a therapeutic effect. Simply initiate the conversation by saying, "You know, we never really talked about what happened four weeks ago. So tell me (again): Exactly what happened when your friend was accidently hit by the car?"

If you see that repeated debriefing conversations over the next few weeks do not begin to alleviate her symptoms of anxiety, then perhaps you should consider having her evaluated by a child specialist to prevent any long-term emotional scarring.

My 9-Month-Old
Does Not Sleep Through the Night

My daughter is nine months old and does not yet sleep through the night. When I get up to feed her, I am so exhausted the next day that it is difficult for me to function. If I ask my husband to feed her, which he is willing to do, he has the same problem and cannot concentrate at work.

Since this is our first child, we do not have any prior experience to guide us.

I've discussed this with my mother. But she was not too helpful. She laughed and told me that she got up in the middle of the night for me and all of my siblings and now it is my turn to do the same. My mother-in-law is no longer living, so I cannot ask her what to do.

I am somewhat uncomfortable discussing this matter with my friends because I do not want to appear incompetent and because I would not want to sound like I am complaining.

When I asked our pediatrician, he recommended that I give the baby a bottle with water, only. He said that way, she will soon learn that it is not worth her while to get up at night. Then she will start sleeping through until morning.

I did try to follow that advice a few times but my baby starting screaming as soon as I placed her back in her crib. I did not have the heart to let her cry like that so I went back and gave her some formula.

I know all newborns wake up at night to be fed. But my husband and I can't take much more of this. Is there anything you can recommend to help us deal with this problem?

I happen to agree with your pediatrician on this one. By approximately 6 months old, most newborns have sufficiently large stomachs to hold enough food after their last feeding to carry them through most of the night. If so, then why is your baby waking up every night demanding to be fed?

The problem here is not that your baby is starving in the middle of the night. A 2- or 3-month-old, perhaps; but not a nine-month-old.

The problem is that you have *trained* your daughter to wake up every night. By feeding her when she wakes up, you and your husband have been rewarding her for disturbing your sleep. For a baby to receive a warm bottle of formula in the middle of the night is the equivalent of an adult getting a paycheck. Inadvertently, therefore, you are reinforcing the very behavior you are seeking to eliminate.

In order to teach your daughter that it is not worthwhile to get up in the middle of the night, you are going to have to follow your pediatrician's recommendation. Picking up your daughter, holding her, and giving her a bottle of water will provide enough soothing reassurance to calm her and eventually get her back to sleep. But it will not provide enough incentive for her to continue waking you each night. A strictly enforced midnight menu of water, only, should train your daughter to sleep through the night in less than a week.

The reason this prescription is difficult to follow for many parents is because children sometimes "insist" on getting the formula. They may refuse to go back to sleep, get up again an hour later, or may even refuse to take the bottle with only water. When that happens, some parents begin to feel guilty. They question whether or not they are doing the "right thing." And their feelings of compassion for their screaming infant may even cloud their judgment.

According to the Vilna Gaon, *ztz"l*, in *Even Sheleimah* (Chap. 6, Note A) the following *pasuk* refers to such parents, "The hands of compassionate women have cooked their own children" (*Eichah* 4:10). Applying this *pasuk* homiletically to parenting, the Vilna Gaon states that the misguided compassion of parents who resist setting limits will ultimately cause detriment to their own children.

Certainly parents should empathize with their child and should try to feel his pain. That is an expression of love and makes the child feel cared for. Even with compassion, however, there can be too much of a good thing. And when parental feelings of sympathy for their crying infant motivates them to go against the pediatrician's recommendation, that is not in the child's best interest.

Yes, it is difficult to sit by and listen to your child cry, especially when you know that she could be so easily satisfied. But you must bear in mind that you are not withholding midnight feeding for purely selfish motives. It is not simply to enable you and your husband to get a good night's sleep. Learning to sleep through the night is in your daughter's best interest, as well.

Your daughter needs parents to care for her during the day who are fully rested. As long as you continue to get up in the middle of the night that will not be possible.

Your daughter also needs a good night's rest. Waking up in the middle of her sleep each night is robbing her of the full rest she needs. For children as well as adults, uninterrupted sleep is more restful than sleep that is disturbed.

Finally, sleeping through the night is the first of many developmental milestones your daughter must pass in order to grow up. Delaying any developmental task could delay her timetable for maturation.

The initial week of implementing this plan will undoubtedly be stressful for all three of you. Your daughter will not surrender her midnight meal without a struggle. She may scream louder and longer than she ever has. You may lose more sleep than you have been missing up until now. And, if you live in a building with thin walls, your neighbors may even complain about the noise.

Hopefully, however, now that you understand why this is so important for your daughter, you and your husband will have the determination to help the three of you clear this developmental hurdle so that you can all get the full night's sleep you all must be needing so desperately by now.

My 4½-Year-Old Sucks His Thumb Throughout the Day

> I purchased a thumbguard to place on my 4½-year-old's thumb to stop his habit of thumb-sucking. He is interested in wearing it, as I promised him a set of traintracks if he stops sucking his thumb (which he does all day and parts of the night).
>
> I know that you cannot take something away from a child without providing him with alternatives. Are there any suggestions you have when we start this program? I worry that we are taking away a source of comfort for him.

Thumb-sucking is an extremely normal behavior for infants and toddlers. It represents a handy, self-soothing, tension-reliever similar to daydreaming or fantasizing in adults.

By age 4 or 5, most children have given up thumb-sucking on their own. As your son is 4½, however, it is understandable that you are concerned about his round-the-clock attachment to his thumb.

As a general rule, it is often best for parents to allow their children the leeway to master developmental tasks whenever they are ready to do so. Pushing them before they are ready can add unnecessary stress that would only be counterproductive.

Because your son is still so heavily engaged in thumb-sucking at this age, however, it is a good idea for you to become more proactive for two reasons.

First, there could be physical consequences of his continued thumb-sucking. As the Torah warns us, "U'sh'mor naf'sh'cha m'od," and, "V'nish'martem m'od l'naf'shoseichem" (*Devarim* 4:9,15). And according to Dr. Stanley Sussman, a highly respected dentist practicing in Boro Park for 40 years, "Thumb-sucking is a noxious habit because it causes the upper teeth to flare forward. If it continues when permanent teeth come in, it can even cause problems requiring orthodontic treatment."

A second reason for wanting to help your son reduce his thumb-sucking is the social repercussions of this behavior. By now, your son is probably attending a preschool program. Whether he is in a play group, nursery or kindergarten class, he is spending a good portion of his day with peers who have almost all eliminated their daytime thumb-sucking. Therefore, he may be teased or ridiculed by his classmates, which we would certainly want to avoid.

Due to these negative consequences of thumb-sucking, many parents today get their children started on the use of a pacifier from infancy. The use of a pacifier allows greater control for the parents. For example, it can be withheld at certain times, such as during the day. In addition, it can be withdrawn gradually until it is completely eliminated, thereby minimizing the stress to the child. For any subsequent children, therefore, you might want to consider the use of a pacifier.

A word of caution, however, must be added. There is also a downside to using a pacifier. If a child has become used to sucking on a pacifier and then the pacifier is lost, a minor calamity can result. The child, for example, may refuse to go to bed, or if in bed, may refuse to go to sleep.

For that reason, it is wise to keep several spare pacifiers readily available for those late-night emergencies when the regular pacifier cannot be found and all drugstores are closed. I am always inspired by the enormous list of gemachs published or posted in the frum neighborhoods in Eretz Yisrael. And by far my "favorite" is the tsumi (pacifier) gemach which comes to the rescue, quieting the midnight madness, when a pacifier is misplaced.

Even though your son has expressed interest in wearing the thumb-guard, I would not recommend you use it for the following reasons. He has probably expressed interest in it only because of the traintracks you have promised him. The thumbguard is a more drastic measure that represents a form of coercion even if your child accepts it.

Furthermore, the message you send by using the thumbguard is that you are trying to eliminate the thumbsucking overnight. That is setting the bar too high and you are absolutely justified in being worried about using it.

As with all behavior-modification projects, we must always keep in mind the wisdom of Chazal: "If you try to accomplish too much [too soon], you will achieve nothing. If you try to accomplish a little [at a time], you will succeed" (*Rosh Hashanah* 4b).

When parents expect too much from their child, they instill frustration and hopelessness in him. As a result, the child could eventually even give up trying. And when that occurs, the parents may wonder why their child lacks motivation, not realizing that they caused this problem by their unrealistic expectations.

I recall, for example, a middle-aged man with whom I was working several years ago. At one point in the therapy, he confided to me that he was unable to learn at a *shiur*, with a *chavrusa* or on his own. As the son of a prominent rav, he was embarrassed by this aberration from an otherwise *frum* lifestyle and he sought my help in overcoming this impasse.

A few weeks later, this man went to visit his parents, something he did on a regular basis. This time, however, he ventured up to the attic and began rummaging through some old papers. To his amazement, he found two of his *Gemara* test papers from elementary school with grades "98" and "100" on them. He was surprised because he had always thought of himself as a "dummy" in *limudei kodesh*.

This man brought the two test papers downstairs and showed them to his elderly father. The father looked at both thoughtfully and then asked, "How come you only got a '98' on this one?"

The son replied, "You know, Ta, I think that's exactly what you said when I brought these papers home the first time."

Eventually, this man succeeded in overcoming his mental block to learning and even helped his own son complete a *seder* of *mishnayos* in time to make a *siyum* at his *bar mitzvah*. But this case dramatically illustrates how much damage can be caused — however well intentioned — by setting unrealistically high standards for children to reach.

I would suggest, therefore, that you begin your behavior-modification program by asking your son to refrain from thumb-sucking *only* during the day *in public*. If he succeeds for a week without relapsing, give him a small reward. If he makes it through four weeks, then give him the traintracks. Only after he has mastered that should you even attempt to eliminate daytime thumb-sucking in private. Nighttime thumb-sucking need not be mentioned now at all, as it will gradually diminish on its own once he has gained control during the day.

How Do I Explain to My 4½-Year-Old Son Why Some Bnei Torah Smoke?

Last week, I was walking with my 4½-year-old son as we passed an obviously *frum* man who was smoking. My son tugged at my arm and asked, "What is that *tatty* doing?"

I was a bit flustered and caught off guard. I did not want my son to admire or aspire to smoking. So I disparaged the stranger by saying that he was acting like a baby.

With hindsight, however, I'm not sure I gave him the best answer. On the one hand, I do not want my son thinking that there is anything cool about smoking. And even though he's not yet 5, I still want him to understand that smoking is detestable. On the other hand, I also want him to respect *bnei Torah*, even if they do smoke. But since we live in a very *frum* neighborhood, the only smokers he ever sees are *bnei Torah*.

As my son is our oldest child, I have never had to deal with this issue before. And I would appreciate any insight you could offer.

Whenever a child asks you a sticky question, you have three choices. You could sidestep the question by distracting the child. You could answer in a way that puts you more at ease, even though your reply may include some dishonesty. Or, you could simply tell the truth. Let's examine the consequences of each option.

If you avoid your child's question, you send him the following message: Whenever you need information about a sensitive or taboo subject, consult your friends, and do not ask me. Clearly, that is not a lesson you ever want to teach your child.

If you answer in any way which could be considered fraudulent, you teach your child not to trust you. And which parent would knowingly send that message to his or her own child?

By process of elimination, therefore, we must arrive at the conclusion that telling the truth is the best approach to answering controversial or touchy questions.

Using the above as a template, how should your response be assessed? Saying that the smoker was "acting like a baby" was not an honest reply. It is not as if the man had been sucking his thumb as he walked down the street. Furthermore, your son will eventually discover that smoking is not really a sign of immaturity. And when he comes to that realization, he will conclude that you are not always a reliable source of accurate information.

What, then, would be a better response to your son's question?

First you should have given him a factual explanation of what the man was doing, such as, "He is smoking a cigarette." An avalanche of questions would undoubtedly follow. Each should be answered honestly, concretely, and on a level appropriate for his intellect.

Then, and only then, should you introduce value judgments, such as, "Isn't it sad that it is so hard for him to stop that he still smokes? I'm sure he would want to stop because it is so unhealthy for him and his family. Let's daven to Hashem that Hashem should help him to be able to stop smoking real soon, O.K.?"

Responding in that way enables you to use this experience as an opportunity to teach concern and caring for a fellow Jew in an unfortunate circumstance. You are then turning his question into a golden *chinuch* opportunity.

Harav Shmuel Miller, *Rosh Hayeshivah* of Yeshiva Bais Yisroel in Brooklyn, once shared with me that his father, Harav Avigdor Miller, *ztz"l*, used to turn everyday events into *mussar* lessons. One summer afternoon, for example, when Harav Shmuel Miller was about 9 years old, he and his father were picking blueberries in the bushes behind their bungalow. An announcement came over the public-address system of the hotel adjacent to their bungalow.

"Before checking out of the hotel," the anonymous voice boomed, "will Mr. _____ please come to the office. Thank you."

"Did you hear that?" Harav Miller, *ztz"l*, asked his young son. "Do you know what that means? That means that someone is being reminded to come to the office to pay his bill before leaving the hotel. And this . a reminder for us, as well. This should remind us that someday we will leave the hotel which is *olam hazeh*. And when it is time for us to leave, we will also have to go to the 'office' of the *Melech Malchei Hamelachim* to settle our account."

Finally, your letter touches on a much broader issue which all parents need to address with their children at some point. You wrote that you want your son "to respect *bnei Torah*, even if they smoke." What you are really saying, therefore, is that you want your son to understand the fundamental truth that even good people can do bad things.

Our ancestors mentioned in the Torah were such spiritual giants that we cannot begin to fathom their greatness. Although the shortcomings they exhibited were far more minuscule than they seem, the Torah's message is clear. Even great people can make mistakes.

Yehudah's declaration, for example, "*Tzadkah mi'meni*, She [Tamar] is more righteous than I am" (*Bereishis* 38:26), will go down for all times as the quintessential admission of error. And on this *pasuk Chazal* teach, "Yehudah, who publicly sanctified Hashem's Name, merited that [within] his name is the [full] Name of *Hakadosh Baruch Hu*" (*Sotah* 10b).

Some parents unfortunately assume that they must be seen by their children as all perfect all the time. They are terrified of revealing any weakness or imperfection to their children. As a result, they find it impossible to ever apologize to their children if they act in a way that they later regret. Somehow they believe that it will harm their children to discover that they are also human beings capable of making mistakes.

The fact of the matter is that it is extremely *beneficial* for children to see that their parents are capable of admitting their own errors. It sets an example for children of how they can cope with their own imperfections without being crushed by them. And in the end it enables the children to respect, admire, and love their parents even more.

Avi (not his real name) talks freely today about his difficult childhood growing up with a perfectionistic, short-tempered father. "How could I get along," Avi asks rhetorically, "with a father who proudly announced all the time, 'I never met a man who could prove me wrong!' " Now that Avi is married and has a family of his own, he makes a point of visiting his widowed father as infrequently as possible.

I am not endorsing or condoning Avi's behavior. Whether parents did a good or not-so-good job raising their children, they are still deserving of respect as mandated by the Torah (*Aseres Hadibros*).

My point in citing Avi's example, however, is to illustrate that all behavior has consequences. And the result of Avi's father's inability to admit mistakes, always assuming and declaring that he was right, was that Avi chose later in life to avoid his father. While I'm sure his father had good intentions, the impact of his parenting and personality styles was to distance his son. He may have thought he was being a perfect role model. In reality, however, he was giving Avi a clear example of how *not* to deal with his own children when he becomes a father.

Returning to your son, you must convey to him — and it is certainly not too late to revise your original explanation — that *bnei Torah* are deserving of respect. They are still capable of blundering at times. And one mistake that far-too-many *bnei Torah* have made was to begin smoking in the first place.

Our 4-year-old
Just Started Bed-Wetting

We have two children, a boy who just turned 4 and a girl who is 15 months old.

Our son has been toilet trained for almost two years. The whole process was quite smooth and uneventful. Considering the horror stories we had heard from our friends, we really got off easily.

Since he was toilet trained, our son has not had any "accidents." Although we were warned to expect some after his sister was born, we were pleasantly surprised that he remained dry even at night.

Recently, however, we have encountered a setback. And we do not know what to make of it or how to handle it at this point. We are, therefore, turning to you for guidance.

About four weeks ago, our son had an accident at night. When he told us about it the next morning, he gave us a long-winded and dramatic "explanation" as to why it happened. As we were concerned that this should not repeat itself, we both made it clear to our son that we were disappointed in him. He seemed to be sufficiently bothered by our disapproval so that it would not happen again.

About two weeks later, he had another accident, also at night. At that point, we were worried that he may be getting used to the idea of wetting his bed at night and we wanted to nip this in the bud, so to speak. So we both reprimanded him. And we told him that if this happens again, he will have to wear diapers when he goes to sleep like his younger sister. He was visibly upset and pleaded with us not to make him wear diapers.

We thought we had succeeded in overcoming the problem until this week when it happened again. This time we told him that we were going to have to speak with someone (you) for advice on how to handle this matter. He then became so distressed that we had to promise we would not use his name in order for him to calm down.

At this point, we are convinced that we need professional advice and we are hoping you can help us.

**First,** I must congratulate you both for having the good judgment to realize that your approach was not working. So often parents assume that their strategy is correct and the only reason they are not getting the desired results is that they have not adequately implemented their plan. Then they persist — sometimes for years — down the wrong parenting path until the damage is irreversible.

Next, I must point out that in describing your son's situation, you used the correct word but may not have understood its full implications. According to *Webster's Dictionary*, an accident is "something occurring by chance or without intention." And a 4-year-old wetting his bed once in two years certainly qualifies as an accident.

In your response to the initial occurrence, however, you did not treat it as "without intention." According to your letter, you "made it clear that you were disappointed in him." That display of disapproval, therefore, was misguided and inappropriate, however well intentioned. By showing your son your disappointment, you were giving him the message, "If you had really tried, you could have prevented this. Now you have let us down."

You wrote, "he seemed to be sufficiently bothered." That is probably an understatement. I suspect he felt terrible about the accident, was quite embarrassed, and may even have been devastated by your reaction.

Then, by trying to control that which was not at all in his control to begin with, he probably became anxious and worried that the situation should not recur. And when it did — which at that point was probably inevitable — your response to his second accident only compounded the problem. By scolding him and threatening to embarrass him even further, he probably added feelings of resentment onto the heaping pile of shame and guilt he was already feeling. And all of that was a surefire recipe for triggering the third episode.

What you should have done was to heed the words of *Chazal*, "A person should never instill excessive fear in his household" (*Gittin* 6b). Applying this maxim to your situation, you should have treated the initial accident as just that, an accident. You should have comforted your son and not made a big deal out of it. Had you done so, he would not have become anxious or resentful. Then you would have truly nipped this in the bud.

Fortunately, it is not too late. Four-year-olds are remarkably resilient. You can, therefore, and you most certainly should, correct your initial error.

Do not tell your son that you spoke with anyone about this. That will only increase his shame and consequently raise his anxiety level. Instead, tell him that you discussed this with *each other* and you realized that perhaps you came down a bit too hard on him. After all, it was not really something that was under his control. If you can bring yourselves to apologize to him, that would be ideal. It would also be teaching him by example that we can take responsibility for our mistakes and do not have to be perfect all of the time.

Once you have that little setting-the-record-straight talk with him, do not assume the matter is resolved. In all likelihood, there will be at least one more incident of nocturnal bed-wetting in the near future. This will represent an unconscious test.

In other words, your son may not be convinced that your change of heart is sincere and permanent. Are you just singing a different tune temporarily or have you really changed your mindset about this? The only way for him to know for sure is to test you and find out.

The next accident will not be a premeditated, deliberate test. And it may not be a test at all. It may simply represent a residue of the anxiety generated from the earlier incidents which were mishandled. Either way, however, just as night follows day, you should expect another accident some time soon.

Whenever that next accident occurs, you want to be sure to take full advantage of the opportunity to demonstrate to your son what you have learned from this column: that accidents are unavoidable, that they are not a badge of shame, and that you are still as loving and supportive of him as you were before. If your demonstration is successful, then you will have taught your son a most valuable lesson.

When parents adopt a perfectionistic, "no mistake" parenting style, they do their children a great disservice. While these parents may be well intentioned, they nevertheless plant the seeds for future handicaps.

I have treated young adults, for example, who were raised by exacting, critical, and perfectionistic parents. As a result, these young people were often paralyzed by indecision and could not make any commitments because of their pathological fear of failure. In their view, if an option was not perfect it must be a "mistake." And they found themselves constantly feeling stuck.

In order to avoid this parenting pitfall, therefore, you should respond to your son's next accident as follows. "It's O.K., sweetheart. These things happen sometimes. I still love you very much. Come help me take off this sheet so we can give you a nice fresh one for tonight."

Finally, when parents respond to temporary toilet-training setbacks, such as your son's, with this gentle, soft-spoken approach, they practically insure that their child will get back on track quickly and the temporary regression does not become a permanent problem.

My 4-Year-Old Daughter Has Daytime Accidents

This inquiry is regarding Dr. Wikler's recent column about bladder-control accidents. He only dealt with nighttime accidents. What about a child who has daytime accidents and has admitted that the reason he/she has the accident is that he/she was in the middle of a game and tried to hold it in?

It would seem to me that in such an instance, there would be more room for a firm approach. My 4-year-old daughter has had a few recent bladder-control accidents both during the daytime as well as during the nighttime.

I do not express disappointment to my daughter regarding the nighttime accidents because that is obviously not her fault. But regarding the daytime accidents wherein she has readily admitted that she was trying to hold it in because she was in the middle of something, I have indeed expressed to her that it was unacceptable. And, yes, I have even used the "diaper threat."

I am very interested to know what Dr. Wikler thinks about this. If his thoughts differ from mine, please request a full and convincing explanation from him because, in all honesty, I will not be prone to altering my approach unless I can truly see the convincing logic of the other approach.

Thank you very much.

There is much critical information that has been omitted from your letter. For example, you did not give any indication as to the frequency of the accidents. While you did say there were "a few recent incidents," that still leaves the amount vague. If, for instance, your daughter had three accidents in the past two weeks, that would be very different from two incidents in the past three months, even though both situations could be described as "a few recent incidents."

At 4 years old, an occasional accident is quite normal. If there are repeated accidents in a short period of time, then parents should be looking for answers.

A second piece of vital information you omitted was the extent of the accidents. Did your daughter wet herself slightly on her way to the bathroom? Or, did she completely relieve herself in her pants? The former case should be viewed as quite normal for her age while the latter case would, again, require further investigation.

In addition, you did not mention how long ago your daughter was toilet trained. Has she been trained for two years or only six months? It makes a big difference because the shorter the time since she was fully trained, the more likely accidents are to occur.

Furthermore, you wrote that your daughter "admitted that she was trying to hold it in because she was in the middle of [a game]." It would be helpful to know if she was holding it in because she was too distracted or having too much fun. Was she afraid or concerned about some negative consequence of interrupting the game? And, if so, what was she worried about?

Finally, you gave no indication whether or not there have been any recent major events in your family. Illness, death, divorce or any other disruption of normal family functioning can often trigger accidents in children even older than your daughter.

Even without all of that specific information, however, I can still discuss a number of the general parenting issues raised in your letter.

As most parents learn eventually, the use of threats — be they "the diaper threat" or any other variety — are notably ineffective in modifying children's behavior. Just as adults are motivated more by the prospect of positive reward than by the threat of punishment, so too children respond similarly.

Most drivers today, for example, have signed up for E-ZPass because it saves them both time and money. While there are still some drivers who pay tolls in cash, the vast majority are already E-ZPass customers. On the other hand, look how many people today speak on handheld cell phones while driving. Even though it is against the law and heavy monetary fines are issued to drivers who are caught, the practice continues unabated. This is an obvious indication that the "threat" method is ineffective.

Generally, parents use threats when they want to frighten their children into complying with the parents' wishes. The parents may have very good justification for wanting their children to modify particular behaviors. The use of fear as a strategy, however, should not be the first choice, unless the child is about to do something dangerous, such as run into the street. *Chazal* have taught, "Rav Chisda said, 'A man should never instill excessive fear in his household' " (*Gittin* 6b).

If fear is to be avoided, then how should parents attempt to modify children's behavior? *Chazal* answered that question as well. "The Rabbis have taught, 'Forever the left [or weaker] hand should push away [and reject or disapprove] and the right [or stronger] hand should bring close [and reward or praise]' " (*Sotah* 47a).

More specifically, charts with stickers, points or prizes, combined with approval and encouragement, are far-more-effective strategies to eliminate undesirable behaviors than threats or punishment.

Finally, the entire premise of your approach to your daughter seems somewhat faulty. You seem to assume that she does not mind wetting herself at all. Therefore, you are attempting to motivate her to want to remain dry by applying a threat that she will fear and thereby increase her motivation. In other words, you are treating this matter as if it were a simple case of stubbornness that you must overpower in order to gain your daughter's obedience.

I believe that even at 4 years old, your daughter would prefer to remain dry. If she is having so many accidents during the day, as well as at night, then there may be other factors involved here.

Two possibilities need to be considered. First, you must ask yourself if your daughter may be under any unusual amount of stress lately. Has she been traumatized in any way? Even if the trauma occurred a few weeks or months ago, she could still be suffering from it. Whenever a young child, such as a 4-year-old, experiences a trauma, it is extremely common for them to have accidents both during the day, as well as at night.

Even if you do not know of any traumatic events in your daughter's life recently, it is still possible that she has experienced one of which you are unaware. For example, while it is unlikely, it is nonetheless possible that she may have been molested by someone without your knowledge. It would be prudent, therefore, for you to ask your daughter about this.

The second possibility is that your daughter is unconsciously acting out anger or resentment at you for some reason. This complex concept requires further clarification.

When young children, such as your daughter, harbor hostile feelings toward a parent, it is much too frightening and perilous for them to express those feelings openly. Young children do not yet possess the language skills needed to vent such feelings verbally. And it is much too threatening for them to act them out directly.

What ends up happening, therefore, is that these angry feelings tend to become expressed indirectly. While they are not going about it in a deliberate, premeditated fashion, children may act out these subconscious feelings. Generally, this takes the form of some misbehavior that achieves the desired result of annoying the parents.

Combining these two possibilities, therefore, it is entirely possible that the pressure you have placed on your daughter with your threats and disapproval has either made her too worried or has provoked her resentment toward you. In either case, the result may just be the very behavior you are attempting to eliminate, namely, the recent bladder-control accidents.

You need not "see the convincing logic of" the other approach. You could, however, simply try it as an experiment, just to see what happens if you replace your "firm approach," with a more positive, incentive-based strategy. You may be, *b'ezras Hashem*, pleasantly surprised.

In order to implement this approach, you must select both long- and short-term prizes. For example, an edible treat works well for the short term. And a significant toy can be used for the long-term prize.

Then you should inform your daughter that she will receive the treat every day that she remains dry. You can pick the same time every day to make that determination. The long-term incentive would have to be earned with a certain number of consecutive dry days, depending on the size of the toy and the tolerance of the child for delayed gratification. A chart posted in her room can help to keep her motivation high, as she can be constantly reminded of her own progress.

Is Our Flexible Standard of Tzenius Confusing For Our 5-Year-Old Daughter?

My question has to do with how an issue we are facing now with our 5-year-old daughter may have repercussions for her when she gets older. Let me explain.

I grew up in a somewhat more liberal or modern neighborhood where the standards of *tzenius* for young children were more relaxed. I now live in a more right-wing section of Brooklyn where the prevalent standards are quite different. My daughter attends school, therefore, with classmates who wear their dresses below the knee and knee-high socks all year long. While I might not have insisted on that for my daughter at this age, I very much do not want her to stick out or feel different from her friends in any way. So we have pretty much adopted that standard for her as well.

Whenever we go to visit my parents, however, we dress our daughter in clothing which is more compatible with the neighborhood in which my parents live. By doing so we avoid any conflict with my parents who would definitely make an issue of the more right-wing clothing style our daughter wears at all other times.

Recently, when I was dressing her to go to my parents, my daughter complained that the skirt she was wearing was not *tzeniusdik*. I explained to her that there are different standards for different places and what she was wearing was fine for where she was going.

I am wondering, though, if this could prove to be problem for her in the future. When she is a teenager, for example, could she rebel against all standards of *tzenius*? And, is it too confusing for her now to grasp this double standard of *tzenius*?

 **One of the most** confusing things for all young children to learn is what behavior is appropriate for which situation. It takes, therefore, many years of growing up for children to learn what conduct is expected in which setting. That learning process is called socialization.

It is through socialization, for example, that children learn that questions such as, "Why does that woman have an earring in her nose?" and "Why does that man have only one leg?" should not be asked out loud in an elevator. In addition, children learn that bike-riding and ball-playing are activities restricted to outdoors and may not be conducted in the living room. Furthermore, children learn that clothing that may be worn in the backyard or on the ball field during the week may not be appropriate to wear in shul on Shabbos.

Generally speaking, therefore, it *is* confusing for children to learn all of the rules of what is proper for each different situation. It is not *too* confusing, however, for them to eventually absorb all of these rules through the process of socialization.

Regarding *tzenius*, however, you are right to be concerned with the future consequences of your current parenting decisions. When it comes to the standards you set in your home, you want to be sure that you are sending your child clear, unambiguous messages.

We may wear fancier clothing on Shabbos and simpler clothing during the week. The reason is to demonstrate the honor and respect due to that special day. The standards of *tzenius*, however, are absolute and cannot be situationally determined or flexible.

Before *Klal Yisrael* left *Mitzrayim*, they were commanded to ask for gold and silver from their non-Jewish neighbors. They were also instructed to take articles of clothing. Then the *pasuk* specifically states that the *Yidden* should "put [this non-Jewish clothing] on their sons and daughters" (*Shemos* 3:22). Why does the Torah only mention the children and not the adults?

One of the Chassidic Masters once explained that the *mitzrim* wore short clothing. Consequently, it would not have been within the proper guidelines of *tzenius* for the Jewish adults to wear such clothes. The clothing would only be suitable, therefore, for the children to wear. He then cited that *pasuk* as a Torah source for the *mitzvah* of *tzenius*.

 It is not within the rubric of this column to discuss the halachic aspects of *tzenius*. As in all matters of *halachah* and *hashkafah*, you should consult your own rav for guidance. Exactly which standards you should use at what age for your children are questions that can and should be posed to your personal *poseik*.

From a psychological perspective, however, by telling your daughter that there are different standards of *tzenius* for whom you are visiting, you are watering down the importance of this *mitzvah* in her eyes. And you are correct in fearing major problems in this area when she reaches adolescence. She could challenge you then, for example, with, "If I could wear whatever I wanted when we used to visit Bubbie and Zeidie when I was younger, why can't I wear whatever I want now when I go out with my friends?"

In your letter, you posed a parent/child dilemma from the perspective of the parent. It seems to me, however, that you also have another parent/child dilemma from the perspective of the child; namely, your relationship with your own parents.

You and your spouse have chosen the standard of *tzenius* you want for your daughter, based on the neighborhood in which you live and the school your daughter attends. Because you are apprehensive of your parents' reactions, however, you have compromised those standards to placate your parents, who would criticize your "right-wing clothing style." In essence then, you are sacrificing your daughter's *chinuch* to appease your parents.

It is most understandable that you would want to circumvent any contention with your parents. The question you must ask yourself, however, is: At what cost?

For the sake of your child, therefore, I would recommend that you reinforce your conviction to the *tzenius* standards you have chosen. And if you are at all ambivalent about where you stand on this issue, I suggest that you first attempt to resolve your mixed feelings. Then, instead of asking if your child will be confused about the current double standard of *tzenius* you have adopted, you should be asking how you can deal more effectively with your parents' criticism of your daughter's more modest clothing.

You could tell your parents, for example — in the most respectful tone of voice, of course — that they had the prerogative to decide how they wanted to dress you and your siblings when they were young parents. Now that you are a parent, you would like to exercise the same privilege. Furthermore, you might add, the wholesale abandonment of modesty in the larger society today makes it much more necessary for your daughter to dress in a more conservative style than when you were growing up. Although your parents may not agree with your decisions, they cannot deny your license to make them. And you owe it to your daughter to exercise that right with conviction.

How Soon Do I Start Visiting My 3½-Year-Old Who Lives With His Mother?

My wife and I separated recently. And we are now in the process of making the final arrangements for the *get*.

We have two children, a 3½-year-old boy and a 5-month-old girl. Both children are currently with their mother at her parents' home.

So far, I have received a lot of advice from family and friends about how I should be dealing with the children. I am not so sure, however, if all of that advice is correct. And that is why I am writing to you.

My main question now has to do with visitation. Some people have told me that I should not be visiting the children now because it will confuse them. The youngest is only an infant but the older one will wonder why I am not around like before. He will see me come and go and not understand what all this means. According to these people, it would be better for my son if I wait until things are finalized before I start coming to see him.

From my perspective, I would like to see my children because I miss them. But I would not want to do anything that will upset them in any way. So I am wondering what you would recommend that I do.

First, let me congratulate you for making the decision to reach out for a "second opinion." So often, people simply accept the advice they are given by well-intentioned friends and relatives without any hesitation. Unfortunately, that advice is not always the best course of action to take.

Studies have shown that as early as a few weeks old, infants can recognize their own mothers. Fathers, however, are a different matter. At 5 months old, therefore, your daughter may still not be able to distinguish you from any other male. So if you do not visit her for a few weeks, now, it will not make much difference to her.

Your son, however, at $3^1/_2$, not only recognizes you but has already bonded with you emotionally. For him, therefore, the separation from you will be most traumatic.

Your friends and relatives are correct that your visits to him now will be very confusing for your son. Why are you not staying like you used to do? he will wonder and may even ask. Why do you not sleep over with the rest of the family? Where are you living now? And why are you not all together as you were in the past?

This confusion will definitely upset him. He may ask you and/or his mother many questions about this. Or, he may keep all of the bewilderment inside, appearing on the surface as if he does not even notice the dramatic changes that have taken place in the family.

Not visiting your son now, however, is not a viable solution. Just because your son does not see you does not mean he is oblivious to your absence. The immediate pain of your coming and going may be lessened. The long-term emotional damage, however, will be greatly increased.

Not visiting your son now will make him feel abandoned by you. He could blame himself for this, thinking, *If I had been a good-enough boy, my father would have still come to see me.*

Even if you resume contact in a few months, or even weeks, the damage to his trust of you will be difficult to repair. He may always harbor the worry that you might "disappear" again. As a result, he may not be able to connect and bond fully with you as he grows up.

By way of analogy, let me point out the following. During infancy, your children were given a wide array of inoculations and immunizations by their pediatrician. In each case, the needle hurt them and they cried from the pain. No responsible parent would even think of "protecting" their children from this pain by refusing to allow them to be vaccinated. The brief discomfort of the injection pales in contrast to the suffering the children would endure if, *challilah*, they were infected with any of the diseases prevented by the shots.

While visits to your son will upset him, if you spare him that discomfort, today, by postponing the start of your visitation, you will cause him much greater suffering down the road.

Longitudinal studies have demonstrated that in order for children to successfully accommodate to their parents' divorce, it is critical for them to maintain regular, continued, and ongoing relationships with both parents. Furthermore, good self-esteem, especially for boys, is directly correlated with a solid father-child relationship maintained through regular visitation. (See, for example, J. Wallerstein and J. Kelly's, *Surviving the Breakup*, Basic Books, 1980.)

I recommend, therefore, that you do everything you can to resume regular contact with your children immediately. And then make sure you maintain that contact on the most consistent basis possible.

The Gemara tells us that, "Whenever a man divorces his first wife, even the *Mizbei'ach*, the Altar in the *Beis HaMikdash*, sheds tears for him" (*Gittin* 90a). The *Mizbei'ach*, of course, is not the only source of tears following a divorce. In addition to the tears of the husband, the wife, and their respective families of origin, the children of the divorcing couple tend to shed the most tears. And the younger the child at the time of the divorce, the more painful is the dissolution of his or her family.

I recall one particular young couple that went through a divorce over 30 years ago. The wife brought her oldest child, a 6-year-old boy, to me for psychological evaluation. When I asked what prompted her to come, she related the following episode that had taken place a few days before she called.

Her son began crying one night and refused to go to sleep. He complained that he wanted his father and could not sleep without him. After numerous failed attempts to calm him down, the woman reluctantly called her ex-husband and asked if their son could sleep with him that night.

The ex-husband agreed and brought the boy back to his home. As he was putting his son to bed, the boy began crying, demanding to return to his mother. Initially, the father refused. Eventually, however, he gave in and returned his son to his ex-wife.

As the father turned to leave, the boy grabbed his father's ankles and begged him not to go. In an emotionally wrenching ordeal for everyone, the father had to literally tear himself away as the boy sobbed bitterly on the floor.

The young mother explained to me that she was concerned that her son's behavior may have indicated some pathological indecision or emotional disorder that might require therapy. And that is why she wanted me to see him.

After conducting the evaluation, I found the boy to be above average in intelligence, emotionally well adjusted and healthy. At the time, I had a poster in my office with a list of sentences all beginning with, "If a child lives with . . . he learns to . . ." The boy read the sign and asked me which of the sentences applied to him?

"What do you live with?" I asked him.

"I live with a mother and father who are separated," he replied.

"And if a child lives with a mother and father who are separated," I asked, "what does he learn to be?"

He thought for a moment and gave me an answer I remember as clearly as if it were yesterday. He said, "He learns to be sad."

When I met again with the mother, I shared with her my findings and repeated that interchange with her son. Then I assured her that her son did not need therapy. He simply needed his mother and father living together.

In conclusion, therefore, I recommend that you not wait to visit your children. You should resume visitation as soon as possible. And make sure that you see them as regularly as possible. In the long run, that will be best for both of them and prevent emotional problems down the road.

2 Elementary School-Age Children

How Can We Prevent Last Year's Afikoman-Deliberation Fiasco With Our 11-Year-Old Daughter From Recurring This Year?

As our Pesach preparations swing into high gear, my wife and I are trying to figure out how to avoid last year's fiasco at our *seder* table.

We literally had a full house. My in-laws are no longer able to make Pesach in their home, so they come to us for the entire *Yom Tov*. And my sister and her husband, who live within walking distance, came to us for the first *seder*, together with their seven children. Including our five children, therefore, there was a total of 18 people at the table.

As my father, a"h, used to do, I hide the *afikoman* at the start of the *seder* and then negotiate its return with whichever child finds it. In addition, I usually offer a smaller prize to all of the other children at the *seder* as well, so they will not feel left out.

Last year, my 11-year-old daughter, who is the second oldest of our children, found the *afikoman*. At the end of the *seudah*, when it came time for the negotiations, she became very uncooperative. First, she pretended not to remember where she put it. Then she tried to stall, saying she needed more time to decide what she wanted. When she finally agreed to begin bargaining, she asked for roller blades!

That was not the first time she had mentioned her desire for roller blades. Five months earlier, she had asked for that to be her birthday present. At that time, my wife and I had explained to her that we did not feel it is appropriate for a Bais Yaakov girl to be roller blading in public. In addition, we do not feel it is safe. And, finally, even if she would wear protective gear and only use them in a park, we feel she is much too young.

When she brought up the roller blades at the *seder*, I calmly repeated our objections. I then asked her to pick something else, as roller blades were completely out of the question.

At that point, our daughter burst into tears and began challenging me in front of everyone. She complained that I was being "unfair," as "everyone knows" that an *afikoman* present is supposed to be something that a child would not otherwise receive. She insisted that was the only thing she wanted. And then she accused me of showing favoritism to her older sister who had found the *afikoman* the year before and extracted our (reluctant) consent for her to have her ears pierced.

Both my wife and I felt very embarrassed by the fuss our daughter made in front of the entire extended family. And it put a major damper on the festive atmosphere that had prevailed up until that point.

Now we are trying to figure out what we can do to prevent a similar debacle from taking place this year when it comes time to haggle over the return of the *afikoman*. What would you recommend?

I can well imagine how upset you both were last year. You and your wife, however, were not the only ones who were embarrassed at the *seder*. Certainly your daughter must have experienced some humiliation, as well, otherwise she would not have been brought to tears. Moreover, all of the other family members must have felt varying degrees of discomfort by witnessing such an open display of raw emotions.

You are to be congratulated, therefore, that you are looking ahead to this year's *sedarim*, trying to modify your behavior to avoid an encore of last year's performance. As *Chazal* have taught, "Who is wise? He who can anticipate future [developments]" (*Tamid* 32a).

What you need to understand is that all disappointment — whether it is experienced by adults or children — represents the difference between expectation and reality. The more highly inflated the expectations are, the deeper the crash of disappointment will be.

Your job now, therefore, is to minimize your children's expectations for their *afikoman* prize. Be sure, however, that you not add to your second daughter's shame by making specific reference to her confrontation with you last year. Simply begin by stating to all of your children, preferably during the relaxed atmosphere of a Shabbos *seudah*, that you want to clarify some ground rules for this year's *afikoman* negotiations.

Explain to your children that the *afikoman* prize is not a carte blanche to be used to bypass any of the standards or rules of your home. It is, rather, a modest incentive to pique interest and attention throughout the proceedings that can become tiresome for young children. Then let your children know what the guidelines are for what you *will* allow. You might give them a category of item (i.e., clothing, toy, *sefer*, etc.) or a dollar amount that will serve as a limit.

Two years ago, when you gave in, albeit reluctantly, to your oldest daughter's wish for pierced ears, you unwittingly sent the wrong message to your children. You signaled to them that *afikoman* negotiations are an opportunity to skirt parental authority. So when your second daughter found the *afikoman* last year, she naturally assumed that she would be able to parlay it in the same way for herself. When you denied her that chance, she understandably felt hurt, disappointed, and even resentful.

My friend and colleague, Rabbi Yaakov Salomon, has a remarkably poignant *afikoman* story, entitled, "Passover: It's All About Listening," in his latest, best-selling book, *Salomon Says* (Shaar Press, '09). In that true story, Salomon paints the painful picture of another *afikoman* catastrophe similar to yours.

A number of years ago, one of Salomon's friends, "Mark" (not his real name), was conducting the *seder* in his home surrounded by family and friends. As Mark was an up-and-coming workaholic swiftly climbing the partnership ladder at a highly prestigious law firm, he was relishing this quality time with his children.

When the moment arrived to negotiate the return of the "stolen" *afikoman*, all eyes turned to 7-year-old "Alex" as he tentatively approached his father.

"Tell me, Alex," Mark began, softly. "What do you want?"

"I want two things, Tatty."

"O.K., Alex. Tell me, what is the first thing?"

"I want *Mashiach* to come, now."

Breathing a sigh of relief, Mark nodded with pride. "I share your wish, Alex. Now, tell me, what is your second wish?"

There was a long, uneasy pause. Everyone at the table leaned forward to be able to hear Alex's next request.

"I, um, I wish . . . your office would burn down."

To his credit, Mark was able to get past his embarrassment to hear the wake-up call and read between the lines of his son's comment. He understood the toll his lifestyle was taking on his family. And a few weeks later, he gave notice at his firm and went to work for a nonprofit organization, utilizing his talents for the community and investing more time with his family.

Mark turned his *afikoman* disaster into a learning experience. And he exploited the full opportunity that it presented to grow as a parent. If you learn the lesson from the *Gemara* cited above to prepare in advance for upcoming parenting challenges, then you, too, will grow from your *afikoman* fiasco last year.

Why Don't Fathers and Sons Talk to Each Other on Their Way to Shul?

This past Shabbos morning I was walking to shul by myself. (All of my children are married now and have their own homes.) During my short (seven-minute) walk to shul I passed four pairs of fathers and sons, also walking to shul, in addition to many individual shul-goers like myself.

What struck me as I passed the fathers and sons was that not one of the pairs were talking to each other! Of course, there can be a brief pause in any conversation. But to see all four pairs walking together in silence just when they passed me or crossed my line of vision appeared to be more than just a coincidence.

When my children were younger, there never seemed to be enough time on the way to shul for us to fit in all we wanted to say to each other. And I recall looking forward to that quality time with them during which there were no distractions whatsoever.

Do you feel my sample was skewed and not at all representative of today's fathers and sons? Am I being overly critical of the younger generation? Or, do you find that there is a problem today of a lack of closeness between fathers and sons? And could that have something to do with all of the "kids-at-risk" business that we read so much about nowadays?

I would like to tell you that you are making a mountain out of a molehill, that your inference drawn from the single experience you described is incorrect and that the problem you perceive between fathers and sons today simply does not exist. Unfortunately, I cannot do so because your observation is right on target.

The scene in your neighborhood on Shabbos morning is repeated in many *frum* areas across the country and perhaps in other countries, as well. At least with the pairs you observed, the fathers were walking with their sons, albeit in silence. In other families, fathers and sons do not even walk together. Sometimes the father walks ahead more quickly or the sons lag behind to schmooze with each other or just to dally. Either way, the sons are deprived of a rich opportunity to bond with their fathers.

Fathers are understandably busy these days. With their work and/or learning schedules so overextended, fathers barely have time to even greet their children during the week. On Shabbos, much time is spent — as it should be — in shul and *beis medrash*. The Shabbos *seudos* are, of course, time fathers spend with the family. But the public atmosphere of the Shabbos table does not allow for the more private, personal conversation so essential for establishing a strong father/son relationship.

Mothers are also just as busy as fathers today. Nevertheless, mothers manage to find the time and place to bond with their sons in a way that fathers often do not.

What about all the time fathers spend with their sons learning? Does that not count as quality time? Have not generations of fathers and sons bonded over a *blatt Gemara*?

Certainly learning together can be a fabulous opportunity for fathers and sons to establish a close, warm, and intimate relationship. Whether or not that is the result, however, depends on how that learning is conducted. If the learning takes place in a relaxed atmosphere, without pressure or excessive criticism, it can, indeed, foster a close father/son relationship. But if the learning takes place in a tense or punitive atmosphere, it can create more of a breach than a bond.

Why is it so important for fathers and sons to have a close relationship in the first place? A father is not supposed to be a pal to this son. What is so wrong if there is a certain respectful emotional distance between fathers and sons?

As Harav Shlomo Wolbe, *ztz"l*, wrote in his classic *sefer, Z'riah U'binyan B'chinuch* (Feldheim, 1995, p. 16), "In order to get through the stage of 14-years-old peacefully, a child must be bound to his parents with a warm relationship [starting in the earlier years.]"

When Harav Wolbe used the plural noun, "parents," it is safe to assume that he was referring to both fathers and mothers. And while many mothers may find it easier than their husbands to develop a warm bond with their children, it is essential for every boy to have a close, affectionate relationship with his father.

The *Gemara* states, "Ten measures of conversation came down to the world. Women took nine and one was left for the rest of the world" (*Kiddushin* 49b). Some mistakenly see this as a derogatory comment disparaging women. On the contrary, this quote acknowledges that women are often more articulate, more expressive of emotion, and more comfortable in conversation than men. As a result, many fathers who have the opportunity — such as when they are walking to shul with their sons on Shabbos — do not take proper advantage of it.

Suppose a father would like to engage his son(s) in conversation while they are walking to shul, but he simply does not know how. What should he do then?

He should continue reading, since practical guidelines and concrete suggestions are offered.

Any father who would like to take full advantage of his walks to and from shul with his sons on Shabbos should ask them open-ended, general questions designed to send the message that he is eager to listen to whatever they would like to tell or ask him.

For example, he could ask his son(s), "How was your week?" "Did anything interesting or funny happen in yeshivah?" "What do you usually do at recess each day?" "Who are your best friends in class?" "What would you like to be when you grow up?" "What do you like best about living here in our neighborhood?" "What would you like to do on our next *Chol HaMoed* trip?" or, "Is there anything you are curious about that you would like to ask me but have not yet had the chance? Maybe now would be a good time."

If he demonstrates genuine interest in the lives of his sons by responding to their answers with appropriate follow-up questions, he will arrive at shul well before the conversation has died a natural death. In addition, his sons will look forward to their next walk to or from shul with him. And he, in turn, will enjoy their company, as well. Finally, he will also be taking out the best insurance policy against any of his sons falling off the *derech* or landing in my office.

And if enough fathers follow these suggestions, then the scene you witnessed last Shabbos may, *b'ezras Hashem*, become a decidedly rare occurrence.

Our Sixth-Grade Son Does Not Want Us To Meet With His Menahel

We have a dilemma with our youngest child, a boy, who is in sixth grade. He has always had some minor behavioral issues in yeshivah but nothing so unusual or out of the ordinary.

This week the *menahel* of his yeshivah called and asked me and my husband to meet with him. He said he would prefer not to go into the reason over the phone. He added that it was "not an emergency," and there was "no rush." He said we should call his secretary to schedule an appointment, "whenever is convenient" for us.

When I mentioned this to our son, he put up a big fuss, urging us not to call back to schedule this meeting. Even though he insisted he had no idea why the *menahel* would want to meet with us, he still did not want us to go.

Neither my husband nor I have any intention of avoiding the *menahel*. But, I must admit, we have been procrastinating.

In case you suspect that our son really does know the reason the *menahel* called but does not want to admit it, you should know that our son has never lied to us.

Do you feel we should disregard our son's feelings and meet with the *menahel*? Or, do you feel we should respect his feelings and not go? And, finally, why do you suppose our son is so opposed to our meeting with his *menahel*?

You definitely must meet with the *menahel* ASAP. I recommend that not because I fear a spontaneous *menahel* demonstration outside of my office if I would advise you otherwise, but because it is the right thing to do. First, you must be curious as to what the *menahel* wants to discuss with you. Secondly, it sends the *menahel* a bad message if you dally in scheduling this meeting. Finally, you want your son to understand that you see the yeshivah/parent relationship as collaborative and cooperative, not adversarial.

Meeting with the *menahel*, however, does not mean that you are disregarding your son's feelings. You can still demonstrate your respect for his feelings in two very important ways.

First, you can and should verbally reflect his feelings. For example, you could tell your son, "We know that you would very much prefer that we not meet with your *menahel*, but we feel that it is important for us to hear whatever he has to say."

Secondly, you can and should inform your son that you will be sharing with him whatever the *menahel* tells you. Your son certainly has a right to know what is discussed in a meeting at which he is the focus. Of course, you may omit some details as needed. But he should know now that he can expect a report, not a transcript, of the meeting shortly after you come home.

Finally, I too am baffled as to why your son would be so opposed to your meeting with the *menahel*. My initial hunch was that he was guilty of some behavioral transgression at yeshivah. If he really has no clue, however, that hypothesis must be ruled out.

Chazal teach us, "Do not judge your fellow man until you have reached his place" (*Pirkei Avos* 2:4). As I have been in your son's position, I could speculate that his objections to your meeting his *menahel* may be related to his prior experiences with the *menahel*.

Among the plaques and diplomas that decorate the walls of my office I have hung a framed letter that I encourage many of the parents who consult with me to read. The letter, addressed to my parents, *a"h*, and signed by my seventh-grade rebbi and English teacher, reads as follows: "We find that Meir has been boisterous and rude in both his English and Hebrew classes. Although we have called his attention to this matter, we find he hasn't corrected his behavior . . . Your cooperation will be appreciated."

While I have no recollection of the behavior to which this letter refers — nor did I when my parents, *a"h*, received this letter — I do clearly recall an incident that took place the following year and involved the same rebbi.

One day after lunch, the assistant *menahel* was standing at the microphone trying to quiet down the yeshivah lunchroom before *bentching*. He had already announced "No talking" when I provoked laughter in a classmate with some gesture or facial expression.

"Wikler! Were you just talking?" the assistant *menahel* asked.

"No," was my matter-of-fact reply.

"I want you to see me after *bentching*," he announced, which effectively achieved the silence he was seeking.

After *bentching*, the assistant *menahel* accused me of "lying" to him and took me into the *menahel*'s office. He then explained to the *menahel* that I had just been caught lying. As he had other matters to attend to, he asked the *menahel* to "deal" with me.

The *menahel* did not ask me for my version of the episode. Instead, he launched into a long-winded *mussar shmuess* on *emes*.

When the *menahel* concluded, he said he wanted to speak with my rebbi, "to really get to the bottom of this." It was then that I realized all hope was lost. For some reason, which I never figured out, my rebbi for seventh- and eighth-grades seemed to relish catching and punishing me for the slightest infractions.

The *menahel* then summoned my rebbi to his office. When my rebbi walked in and saw I was in trouble for something, the glee in his eyes was undeniable.

"How has Meir been acting in class lately?" the *menahel* asked.

"I'm very sorry to have to report this. But he has not been behaving well *at all*," my rebbi replied.

"This is important for me to know," said the *menahel*. "Can you give me some examples?"

"Well, I'm really not prepared," my rebbi explained. "Had I known you would be asking, I would have had some examples ready."

"All right, then, just give me one," the *menahel* almost pleaded.

"I'm sure there are others," my rebbi began, "but this is all I can think of at the moment. Whenever I ask the class to line up before we go downstairs to lunch or recess, Meir usually gets on the back of the line."

The *menahel* thanked my rebbi and sent him back to class. He then asked his secretary to call my father, *a"h*, at work. With me on an extension line, the *menahel* told my father that I had been a behavior problem at yeshivah lately, an example of which was my getting on the end of the line before the class went downstairs.

By this time, I had been brought to tears. The *menahel* asked my father to speak to me at home and then apologized for calling him at work. He told me to wash my face and return to class, adding that some day I would thank him for what he had done.

My father did not speak to me about this episode until we were walking to shul on Shabbos morning two days later. "About the phone call I got from your *menahel* this week," he began as my stomach dropped. "I just want you to know that I really do not care where you stand on line at yeshivah. But if it means the *menahel* will call me at work, please do me a favor and get on the middle or beginning of the line. When my secretary said, 'It's your son's principal on the phone,' I almost had a heart attack."

Looking back now, I realize how right the *menahel* was. I really do thank him for giving me such a wonderfully graphic illustration of how *mechanchim* should not behave.

Returning to your original question, let me reiterate that you definitely must meet with your son's *menahel*. When you go – and it should be sooner rather than later – you need not go with a heavy heart. It may be that the *menahel* wants to praise your son, and he prefers to deliver that *nachas* face to face, saying *ashrei yeladito* (happy are the parents who brought him into this world).

Our 12-Year-Old Daughter Resents Our Hachnasas Orchim

My husband and I have always prided ourselves on our open home and our active involvement in the beautiful *mitzvah* of *hachnasas orchim*. We are both *ba'alei teshuvah,* and we each benefited greatly from this *mitzvah* when we were becoming *frum*. And we now see it as an opportunity to give back that which we have received.

Recently, however, I have been having second thoughts about the extent of our involvement in this *mitzvah*. These doubts were triggered by a passing comment our 12-year-old daughter made last week.

She asked if we were having guests for Shabbos. When I told her we were, she rolled her eyes, wrinkled her nose and said, "Sometimes I wish we didn't have so many guests all the time."

Now, we certainly do not have guests "all the time." So that was an exaggeration. But if our daughter feels that way and she is the oldest of our four children, then perhaps our younger children share her discontent. And, if so, are we having guests too often?

On the other hand, I'm not sure if we should stop inviting guests altogether. After all, many of our guests are single and have no other place to go for Shabbos.

How would you advise us to handle this dilemma?

Whether you are *ba'alei teshuvah* or not, we all have an obligation to open our homes to guests. As the *Gemara* teaches us, and as we say each morning following *birchas haTorah*, *hachnasas orchim* is one of six *mitzvos* "whose fruits a person consumes in this world while the principal remains intact for him to enjoy in the World to Come" (*Shabbos* 127a, *Kiddushin* 39b).

Furthermore, it is because we continue to emulate Avraham Avinu by performing acts of *chesed* such as *hachnasas orchim* that Hashem chose Avraham Avinu in the first place. As the Torah relates, "For I know him [Avraham Avinu], that he will command his children and his household [and all succeeding generations] after him, to keep the way of Hashem to do acts of righteousness and justice in order that He [Hashem] should fulfill for Avraham that which He promised him" (*Bereishis* 18:19).

Perhaps Rabbeinu Bachya, one of the *Rishonim*, summed it up best when he wrote, "Whoever grabs onto the *mitzvah* of *hachnasas orchim* will inherit *Gan Eden*" (Rabbeinu Bachya on *Bereishis* 21:33).

We are all equally obligated, therefore, to participate actively in the *mitzvah* of *hachnasas orchim*. Nevertheless, we must never allow the needs of outsiders to take precedence over the needs of our immediate family. The question then becomes: How do we achieve the proper *balance*, fulfilling our dual responsibilities to our family and to our fellow Jews?

The first thing you need to bear in mind is that by inviting guests you are benefiting your children as well as your guests. Children need to learn how to share what they have with others. And this does not come naturally to children.

Some children, however, are even more possessive than others. These children are never willing to share their toys or other belongings with anyone. Parents of such children face a difficult but vital challenge. They must gradually explain to their children that whatever Hashem has granted us was meant to be shared with others. And that is why He gave it to us in the first place.

All children need to learn this important lesson for a number of reasons. First, it will make them more appreciative of whatever they have. And they will be less likely to take their blessings for granted. Secondly, it will discourage them from becoming greedy, selfish, and self-centered — all extremely abhorrent *middos* any parent would want to eliminate from his children. And, finally, it will train them to become *ba'alei chesed* when they grow up.

I heard, for example, of one *frum* family in Brooklyn with many children and limited sleeping accommodations. In order for the zaide to visit for Shabbos, the 8-year-old would have had to give up his bedroom. And because this boy stubbornly refused to do so, his grandfather was never able to come from out of town to spend Shabbos with his family.

Since I did not know this family, I cannot explain why the parents allowed their 8-year-old son to rule the roost. And while it is an extreme example, it does illustrate how far things can get out of hand when parents do not pay proper attention to their children's *middos*.

The second thing you need to consider is that some children feel that the presence of guests at the Shabbos table deprives them of quality time with their parents. When guests are at the table, the parents need to divide their attention in ways that could make high-wire acrobatics look easy by comparison.

Some children feel intimidated by guests. These children may feel somewhat inhibited and unable to bring up questions or topics of conversation that they would more readily do if no outsiders were present. For such children, having guests means that things they had wanted to discuss, relate or ask must be put on hold. And that can be experienced as a most frustrating disappointment.

Just because your daughter expressed that sentiment does not mean that your other children feel the same way. Nevertheless, even if she is the only one of your children who feels that way, her emotional needs should still not be ignored.

In order to help you achieve the proper balance between meeting the emotional needs of your children and fulfilling your obligations of *hachnasas orchim*, I would like to offer two practical suggestions.

First, as you surely know, there are three *seudos* every Shabbos. Instead of having some guests at each meal, you could try to arrange that at least one or two of the *seudos* could be guest-free. That way, your children would have the opportunity to have some undivided attention from you every Shabbos.

If your Shabbos company must sleep over because they do not live in your neighborhood, then they would have to join you for all three *seudos*. In that case, you might have to arrange for some guest-free Shabbosim, so that your daughter will not feel deprived of your attention and resentful of your guests.

If, for whatever reasons, you are unable to arrange for regular guest-free *seudos* or Shabbosim, then you should consider a second strategy to balance the competing needs of your family and guests. You could commit yourselves to some private time with your children after the *seudah* Friday night in the winter or after the Shabbos-day *seudah* in the summer.

Even if you have sleep-over guests, they do not need to be entertained constantly. And you are certainly entitled to learn or schmooze privately with your children after one of the *seudos*.

If your children know, in advance, that they will have this private time with you every Shabbos, during a guest-free *seudah* or after the meal, then they will also learn a valuable lesson by the example you set of how to balance responsibilities in a Torah home.

No discussion of the Shabbos table would be complete without at least calling attention to the touchy subject of children remaining at the table until after *bentching*. In some homes, this requirement is imposed with all of the force of a halachic obligation. In other homes, a more relaxed policy is adopted, allowing children to wander off in between courses if and when they are bored.

Both of these systems have been used successfully in countless homes. It is not for me to endorse one over the other.

What is relevant to the subject of guests at the table, however, is that using the former system, when the parents' attention is focused more on the guests, places an unfair imposition on the children. If parents focus full attention on the children, even when guests are present, then the children can be required to remain at the table until after *bentching*. But if parents are primarily engaged in conversation with the guests and the overlooked children are compelled to remain at the table throughout the meal, they could feel like hostages. And if so, their resentment of your *hachnasas orchim* would be understandable.

What you need to aim for is a proper balance. If you have young children at the Shabbos table, however, you should allow most of the attention to be directed toward them. This will not be at the expense of your not-yet-*frum* guests because you will be providing an excellent example from which they will learn priceless lessons regarding the proper priorities in a Torah home.

Our 10-Year-Old Son Accuses Us Of Hating Him

We have three children, a girl 5, and two boys, 8 and 10. They are all wonderful children, *bli ayin hara*. Our question, however, has to do with our oldest.

In many ways, he could be described as a "model child." Whenever he is out of our home, he makes a marvelous impression on whomever he meets. His teachers and rebbe'im have nothing but praise for his conduct in class. And neighbors and relatives simply cannot get over how well mannered and polite he is whenever they see him.

Our son does not only get along well with adults. He also is well liked and popular among his peers. He has many good friends.

Even at home, our son is well behaved. He is respectful, cooperative, and pleasant. So why are we writing to you?

Our son is certainly not an angel, nor would we want or expect him to be one. He is a normal 10-year-old boy. And as such, he occasionally misbehaves at home, requiring me or my wife to scold him. I should point out that neither of us is abusive or overly harsh, in any way. Nevertheless, regardless of how mildly the reprimand is worded, he typically responds by accusing us of "hating" him.

Both my wife and I are psychologically sophisticated enough to realize that he may be jealous of his younger brother and sister. Certainly no home is immune to sibling rivalry. But the intensity of his complaints do give us pause and make us wonder if there is something we are missing here or if there is something we should be doing about this.

**As the oldest of your three children,** your 10-year-old is undoubtedly the one to be most affected by sibling rivalry for two very important reasons. First, he was the one who was displaced and dethroned most often in the family. Until his younger brother was born, he was an only child, enjoying the full attention from you and your wife. Although he probably cannot consciously recall the birth of his brother, the displacement he felt at the time and his removal from center stage were powerful experiences that can still affect him today. When his sister was born — which he most likely can remember — he went through the reduction of your time and attention all over again.

The second reason your 10-year-old may feel the competition with his siblings more intensely is because he has the bar set higher for him than anyone else. For your daughter to elicit affection or praise from you or your wife, she needs only to look cute or say something funny. Your 8-year-old must perform to a higher standard to earn your approval but still not as high as what you might expect from your oldest. The 10-year-old realizes, therefore, that the most is expected of him. That realization may appear to him to represent an unfair inequality.

As long as things are proceeding business as usual, there is no opportunity or pressing need for him to address any of this with you. When he is receiving the opposite of what he is seeking, however, meaning that he is hearing rebuke rather than praise, his frustration with that perceived unfairness bubbles up to the surface and prompts him to lash out with his stinging indictment, "You hate me!"

You are correct, therefore, in attributing your son's response to the fallout of sibling rivalry. From your letter, there is no indication that you or your wife are doing anything to exacerbate this normal conflict among your children. It does not appear, therefore, that there is anything you are missing.

There is, however, something more you can and should be doing to mitigate the impact of the standard sibling rivalry on your older son. You need to give him some private time.

I have discussed the importance of private, quality time in building self-esteem in children in my first parenting book, *Partners With*

Hashem: Effective Guidelines for Successful Parenting (ArtScroll '00). Private time can also go a long way toward offsetting the feeling of being unloved that sibling rivalry can generate in some children.

In order to be most effective, you should initiate the private time with your son by saying that you are doing this because you feel that you are not spending enough time alone with him. You should set aside a specific amount of time, such as 20 or 30 minutes, on the same day of the week. Make it an appointment that you only reschedule in case of an emergency or a serious conflict.

Let your son know that the agenda for this private time is entirely up to him. While you set the time limit, he decides how the time is used. He could play a game with you, schmooze, go for a walk or build a *shtender*. You should not spend any money on him or go anywhere in the car. The emphasis and focus is on your relationship.

Make sure you do not ever use the private time as a reward or punishment. It should not be conditional on his good behavior or academic performance. The message you are trying to send with private time is that you love your son *unconditionally*. This is a message *all* children need to receive. It is precisely this message that allows children to be corrected and criticized by their parents and *not* feel hated. And it is this message that needs reinforcement whenever a child shows that he is doubting that love, as when your son accuses you of hating him.

Inevitably, you will be interrupted during your private time by your wife, the other children, your cell phone or the doorbell. These should be seen not as annoying interferences but as golden opportunities to demonstrate to your son that he is your priority. Every time you announce, "I'm sorry, I'm busy now," your commitment to him will be demonstrated in very real terms.

You also have to make sure that you start and end on time. If he tries to manipulate "just a few more minutes" from you, you must resist the temptation to be generous and compassionate. If you do add even two minutes today, he will expect that as the new time limit from now on. And then when you are unable to add the "extra time," he will feel cheated, undermining the entire process.

Won't the other children also want "private time" when they see your older son getting it? Yes, they most certainly will. If at all possible, therefore, it would be good for all your children to get some private time.

If that is not practical because of your schedule or the size of your family, then you must explain to your son that he may not flaunt it over his siblings. It need not be a secret. But he still needs to hear from you that if he should laud it over his siblings, it will prevent you from being able to maintain it.

What I have described is a proven strategy to help you solidify your bonds with your son and develop a closer relationship. It involves interacting with your son on a one-on-one basis at a predetermined, consistent time that he can count on and look forward to.

While it is certainly not completely analogous, the parent/child relationship can be compared to the connection our people have with Hashem *Yisbarach*. And the closeness parents need to foster with their children can be likened to the eternal bond between Hashem and *Klal Yisrael*.

We have enjoyed a close, intimate relationship with Hashem for over 3300 years. Hashem has even referred to us as *"segulah mikol ha'amim*, the most beloved treasure of all the peoples" (*Shemos* 19:5). Our unique relationship was demonstrated by Hashem speaking to us in a very private "conversation" at *Har Sinai*. And that was the only time in the entire history of the world that Hashem spoke directly to an entire nation (*Devarim* 4:32,33).

To this day, we still yearn for the revival of that conversation, as we say every Shabbos in the *kedushah* for *Mussaf* (*Sephard* and *Ashkenaz*), "And may He let us hear [His voice] again, in His mercy, before the eyes of every living being."

Our 8-Year-Old Son
Violently Resists Dental Work

My 8-year-old son has always been on the fearful, worrisome side. He took a long time to get used to going to kindergarten and later to day camp. He adjusts poorly to change of any kind. If there is a new bus driver or car pool driver one day, he can get so nervous that he will become nauseous and throw up. And he even resists going to play at friends' homes, preferring them to play at our house.

We have two older children and one younger. None of them enjoy the experience of going to the dentist but they are able to manage it. For our 8-year-old, however, going to the dentist is a major ordeal.

Last year, he made a terrible scene at the dentist's office. He cried and kicked, making it almost impossible for the dentist to check and clean his teeth. I literally had to forcibly restrain my son in order for the dentist to work on him.

When we left the dentist's office last year, the dentist advised me to have my son admitted to the hospital next year so that he could have dental work done under general anesthesia. (The dentist tried laughing gas in his office but it was not at all effective with my son.)

I have heard stories about complications with general anesthesia for such young children. So I am concerned about the risks involved. And my husband and I would prefer to avoid all of the hassles of an overnight stay in the hospital with my son simply for routine dental work.

Why does our son have such a violent reaction to going to the dentist and is there anything which you could recommend that we might do to alleviate some of his intense anxiety about having dental work done?

As has been pointed out in previous articles in this column, all children are born with their own unique personality traits. As a result of their personal DNA, all children start life with their own psychological and emotional endowment. Some children, therefore, are naturally more aggressive, more artistic, more independent, or — as is the case with your son — more predisposed to worry and fear.

Your son's intense fear of the dentist's office, then, may have nothing to do with the dentist, his office or the way in which you have handled his appointments. While you may have had nothing to do with causing the problem, however, does not mean that there is nothing you can do to resolve this predicament.

When children — or adults for that matter — suffer from intense, irrational fear of normal, everyday situations, the treatment of choice is what is called systematic desensitization. This clinical term means that the person suffering from elevated anxiety is presented with gradually increased exposure to the fearful situation.

Take airplane travel, for instance. Adults who suffer from phobic reactions to flying are gradually encouraged to visit airports, visualize boarding a plane, and, eventually, taking a short commuter flight with a therapist coming along for emotional support.

Breaking the goal down into bite-size pieces is the key to success in overcoming such fears. As the individual is subjected to gradually increasing levels of exposure to the feared situation, he or she slowly becomes desensitized, hence the term, "systematic desensitization."

A common form of desensitization is when amateur or professional actors rehearse a performance. The natural stage fright of the players is gradually reduced with each rehearsal until the cast is able to perform on stage without having any anxiety attacks.

Moshe Rabbeinu was on a spiritual level that is far beyond our limited abilities to comprehend. His emotions and behavior, therefore, cannot be compared with our own on any level. Nevertheless, as Rashi repeats in his commentary on *Chumash*, "*Ein mikra sotzei midei p'shuto*, no *pasuk* can be completely divorced from its literal meaning."

When the Torah tells us, therefore, that Moshe Rabbeinu "fled from the snake" (*Shemos* 4:3), after he had followed Hashem's command to throw his staff to the ground (when he had been speaking with Hashem at the burning bush), we may interpret this to mean that some degree of fear may have been present. In fact, the *Sforno*, in his commentary on that *pasuk*, points out that the snake actually pursued Moshe Rabbeinu, thereby causing him to flee.

When this miracle was performed a second time, as Aaron cast his staff to the ground in front of Pharaoh and it turned into a snake (*Shemos* 7:10), there is no indication that Moshe Rabbeinu made any attempt to escape the snake.

While it must be reiterated that the actions and emotions of Moshe Rabbeinu bear no resemblance to our own, that fact should not prevent us from inferring from the *pesukim* quoted above the undeniable truth that repetitive rehearsals can reduce anxiety.

This fundamental reality of human emotions can be harnessed to help you with your dilemma. If you can create a rehearsal of a trip to the dentist for your son, therefore, you may be able to reduce his anxiety level enough for him to get through the experience.

I am not suggesting here that you take your son to the dentist for a trial run before his actual appointment. Seeing the dentist in his office may arouse so much anxiety in your son that it would totally defeat the purpose, even if your dentist would put up with the charade.

What I am suggesting is that you simulate a trip to the dentist at home. In order to do this successfully, you would need the cooperation of other family members. Father could play the role of the dentist. Mother might be the hygienist and/or receptionist. Another sibling should be cast as the patient who is being tended to before your son.

All of this should take place in a relaxed, and if possible, humorous atmosphere of lighthearted playfulness. A reclining chair can be used as the dentist chair and a *nagel vasser* bowl can be used in place of the dentist's sink. A straightened paper clip can be used for the dentist's probe. And an electric toothbrush would recreate both the sound and feel of the dentist's cleaning tool.

Finally, even X-rays can be simulated by using small wheat — I prefer whole wheat, myself — crackers. The dentist (father) can place the crackers inside your son's mouth and ask him to hold them there for the typical few seconds until the beep sounds, after which he can eat the X-ray (cracker), providing that he recited the proper *berachah* before taking it into his mouth.

I recall one family to whom I gave these instructions who were going through a situation similar to yours. That family improvised creatively and had the father wear his *kittel* for the procedure. They reported to me that the entire family really enjoyed the game and could not stop laughing. It helped their son reduce his dentist anxiety. And I hope it helps your son, too.

Which Trip Would Be Best for Our Daughter Who Is Entering Fifth Grade and Going to Sleepaway Camp for the First Time?

We registered our daughter for the second trip of sleepaway camp this summer, which was her choice; but I'm not sure we made the right decision. She is entering fifth grade next year and this will be her first summer at a sleepaway camp. For most of her friends, this will be their second summer at camp. Our daughter, however, did not want to go last year because she was afraid that she would get homesick.

My husband and I are now wondering if it would have been better for us to send her for the first trip. That way, if she does get homesick and has to leave camp, she will still be able to try again for the second trip. What do you think?

Your question demonstrates how you are fulfilling the words of *Chazal* who declared, "Who is wise? He who can anticipate future [developments]" (*Tamid* 32a). It is beneficial that you are asking the right questions now so as to forestall difficulty down the road.

You definitely made the right decision for a number of reasons. First and foremost, your daughter preferred to go for the second trip. Perhaps her friends are going then. Perhaps she has heard that camp is more fun after *Tishah B'Av* than before. Or, perhaps she just believes that she will be less prone to feelings of homesickness during the second trip because she will have spent the entire month of July at home. Regardless of her motives, if she expressed a desire to go for the second trip, it was wise of you to honor her request, especially in light of the fact that this will be her very first experience at sleepaway camp. And, therefore, you want to do whatever you can to make her feel comfortable.

Having said that, however, there is some vital information which you omitted from your letter. More specifically, you did not indicate whether your daughter's friends will be attending both first and second trips or only the second trip. In addition, you did not mention whether any of these friends are close friends with whom she feels especially comfortable.

If her friends are, in fact, going only for the second trip, then it makes perfect sense that she should go along with them. If, however, most of them will be there for the first trip and will be staying on for the second trip as well, then your daughter will be joining them halfway through their camping experience this summer. If so, then all of the events, songs, and lore they will share with each other will be foreign to her. And that could contribute to her feeling "out of the loop," so to speak.

This does not mean you should switch her registration to the first trip. It does mean, however, that you should inquire about which trips her friends will be attending. And if they will be there ahead of her, you should raise this issue with your daughter and discuss it with her. She may wish to stick to her original plan. Or, she may want to reconsider. Either way, you will have done you job of helping her to "anticipate future developments."

Speaking of "future developments," even before you discuss this with your daughter, you should check with the camp to see if switching her registration is even possible. If not, then why open a whole can of worms by getting your daughter interested in an option which is not even available?

Regarding the closeness of her friendships, there is a big difference between a friend and a close friend. Children, like adults, enjoy the company of both. In times of stress, however, such as when one is away from home for the first time for an extended period, it is only a close friend who can really provide the comfort and reassurance that is so desperately needed.

A second reason why I support your decision is that your rationale for doubting your choice is somewhat flawed. You wrote that by sending your daughter for the first trip, you would have the opportunity to try again for the second trip in case your daughter would become so homesick during the first trip that she would need to come home.

You must bear in mind, however, that a camper who suffers such intense anxiety at the separation from parents that she needs to come home before the end of the trip will be too traumatized to even consider the idea of returning two or three weeks later. There would have been no benefit, therefore, to your having switched the registration for the first trip.

Finally, the most important reason the second trip would be best for your daughter this summer is because it will afford you an additional four weeks to help prepare her for the experience. Even though your daughter chose to attend overnight camp this summer, which suggests that she is ready, if she "was afraid that she would get homesick," last year, you must take advantage of the time now, before she leaves, to prepare her for the separation by taking as many of the following steps as you can.

✓ Talk to her about camp. Don't let her push you off or avoid the conversation. Talking about any fear helps us minimize it. Let her know that you are not bringing up the subject because you lack confidence in her ability to handle the separation. Rather, you are initiating the conversation as a kind of insurance policy.

✓ Ask her to anticipate the separation. How does she think she will feel? When does she suspect it will be the most difficult and why? Help her to answer these questions by recalling together previous episodes when she did get homesick.

✓ Discuss strategies for coping. How did she handle her anxieties in the past when she was away from home? What helped at those times? What does she think would help her this summer? Try get her to verbalize her concerns and then problem-solve with her in advance. If, for example, she is worried about not being able to speak with you, try to find out the camp's policy about calling home so you can help your daughter to adjust to it before she gets to camp. If it is feasible for you, bringing your daughter to camp in July to visit and/or meet some of the staff may go a long way toward facilitating her successful adjustment to camp in August.

✓ Introduce mini separations now as a way of building up to the major separation of camp. Encourage an overnight at a friend or relative's home. If she has never spent the night at her grandparents' home without you, now would be an excellent time to try it. Use that visit as a trial run in preparation for camp. Then ask your daughter to pay attention to what triggers her anxiety and what alleviates it, however slightly, while she is away from home.

✓ Prepare letters, photos or other sources of comfort that your daughter can turn to if and when she will need them while she is at camp. One parent with whom I worked many years ago recorded an audiotape of soothing and reassuring messages which he gave to his son the day he left for overnight camp for the first time. His son listened to the tape whenever he felt the first pangs of homesickness and succeeded in remaining at camp throughout the summer and was even sorry to go home when the trip was over.

It is important to remember that many children experience some feelings of homesickness during their first summer at overnight camp. Only a few of them have an especially difficult time coping with the separation. If those more anxious and worrisome children were properly prepared, however — as, hopefully, your daughter will be after you implement the strategies outlined above — many of them would have learned the coping skills needed to successfully manage their anxiety. And, as a result, they would have been able to remain at camp — as I trust your daughter will — for an enjoyable and productive summer.

Our 9-year-old
Is Fearful of the School Bus

For some reason, which my husband and I cannot figure out, our 9-year-old daughter is unable to get on the school bus without putting up a fuss.

Four years ago, when she began Pre 1-A, she also had a difficult time becoming adjusted. Eventually, however, she calmed down and got used to taking the bus to school. Since then, she has *kvetched* a little occasionally. But it has never been as bad as this year.

Some days are better than others. But Monday mornings are the worst. By Sunday night she starts complaining of a stomachache or a headache. The next morning, she has a very hard time pulling herself out of bed and getting dressed. She cannot even eat breakfast because she feels so nauseous. Sometimes she actually throws up just before or as the bus arrives. Then she begins to cry and refuses to get on the bus. At times, my husband and I literally have to pick her up and put her on the bus while she is kicking and screaming.

Both my husband and I work and neither of us has time to drive her to school. If we are forced to take her because she misses the bus, it is a major inconvenience.

She has always been somewhat on the fearful side, resisting doctor visits, avoiding change, declining sleepover invitations from friends, etc. Her difficulty with the school bus this year, however, represents a major setback for her.

Of course, we have asked her why she is so much more fearful of the school bus now than she was last year and the year before. But each time we ask, the answer is always the same: "I don't know."

What could cause a child to have such a reaction to something to which she had already become accustomed? And, do you think she needs some kind of therapy now to help her calm down?

It sounds as if your daughter may be suffering from a classical case of Separation Anxiety Disorder, a common malady among school-aged children in which any separation from parents (especially going to school) will generate abnormally high levels of anxiety.

Separation Anxiety Disorder can be caused by early childhood traumas, prolonged and stressful periods of separation from parents, or incidents of abuse or neglect. In most cases, however, the disorder cannot be traced to any specific environmental factor. Rather, it is caused by the inborn psychological makeup of the child. Some children, therefore, are simply more worrisome, fearful, and anxious than their peers. And your daughter may be one of them.

Even though your daughter seemed to have adjusted to the separation of going to school, it does not take much to trigger a relapse in children who struggle with separation anxiety. A change in routine, making the transition from camp to school, or even a new bus or driver is sometimes all it takes to precipitate a regression.

Your daughter may, indeed, need therapy to help her learn to manage her excessively high levels of anxiety. Before you take that step, however, there are some practical strategies you should employ that are similar to those a therapist would do with her.

First, inform your daughter that you recognize she has a problem with going to school and you are prepared to work with her to help her overcome it. This will give her hope and encouragement.

Next, clarify the goal, which is for her to go on the school bus each morning without any fuss and without needing to be forced. Explain to her that this is a goal that will only be achieved gradually, by whittling down her anxiety level. As *Chazal* have taught, "If you try to accomplish too much [too soon], you will achieve nothing. If you try to accomplish a little [at a time], you will succeed" (*Rosh Hashanah* 4b).

Discuss with your daughter what prize or reward would be meaningful for her to receive when she reaches this goal. Remember, this is not a bribe, to manipulate her compliance. Rather, this is a concrete acknowledgment on your part that the work ahead will be difficult and challenging. And when she achieves the goal, she will have earned the reward.

Finally, arrange with your daughter to have a daily problem-solving session for 10 or 15 minutes, during which you will discuss various exercises and "homework" she can do during the day.

For example, you can have your daughter monitor her own anxiety level throughout the day. When is she most anxious? When is she most calm? What sort of thoughts or situations make her most uncomfortable?

You can also do this exercise with her by "walking her through" the morning routine out loud. Describe the process. Ask her at what point she first feels anxious. When does it get the worst? What is her worst fear at that time?

Another exercise is to ask her to list the situations, things or thoughts that tend to calm her down, even slightly. Which one helps the most? Which one helps the least? Explain to your daughter that thoughts can calm people down the same way they can upset or frighten. Point out to her that her worst-case-scenario *thoughts* about the school bus are what make her anxious. By focusing on calming, reassuring or encouraging *thoughts*, she can begin to take the edge off of her anxiety.

Generally, children cannot come up with any positive or calming thoughts when they are experiencing intense panic, such as when the school bus arrives. They are capable of identifying such positive thoughts, however, when they are faced with milder episodes of elevated anxiety, such as when they feel a longing to be back home in the middle of the school day. Thoughts such as, "It's only two more hours left of school," or, "As soon as I get home, I'll have some milk and cookies," are soothing strategies that can be adapted to the major separation challenge of getting on the bus.

After you have made this list together, write the items down on paper. Give your daughter a copy and tell her to keep it with her. That way, she can refer to it whenever she feels even a little anxious at any time during the day.

This program is time consuming and will require considerable patience on your part. The pride and joy on your daughter's face when she earns her prize and achieves her goal, however, will make it all more than worthwhile. And just in case you need any further encouragement to launch this program with your daughter, let me assure you that I have guided other parents of school-bus-phobic children through these same steps. The successful outcomes they all achieved makes me confident that you and your daughter will also overcome this temporary obstacle.

Could Fear of the School Bus Be a Symptom of Abuse?

Recently, you dealt with a question regarding a 9-year-old who dreads boarding the school bus each morning. Your answer is clear and helpful, with a plan for parents to help their daughter deal with her anxiety. From the many articles on abuse that I've read recently, this newfound fear (even if it seems to be only a newly awakened fear) is one of the "red flag" circumstances that parents should be aware of.

Shouldn't the answer have included advice to the parents to look into the bus arrangements? Is there a bus teacher on duty? Is there a new driver? Is she ever alone on the bus (picked up first or dropped off last)? Is her fear only about boarding the bus, or does it last throughout school hours? Does she fear the bus ride home as well?

I'm wondering if I'm overreacting to a situation from reading so much, or if you have a specific reason or more information from parts of the letter that were perhaps not printed, that caused you to completely discount the possibility of abuse being the reason for this girl's exaggerated fear of boarding the bus.

It happens to be that my niece reported to her school events that were repeatedly taking place on the bus that were unknown to the rest of the riders, except for the perpetrator (a 9-year-old), her victim, and the two girls sitting across the aisle. The perpetrator brought three treats every single day which effectively bought their silence although she never actually threatened them into silence.

The school obviously took the matter seriously because the situation changed immediately. I'm sure they handled the matter with the young abuser and her family. It's a miracle that one little girl had the courage to open up to her mother, and the mother acted responsibly by informing the school instead of ignoring it by telling her own child just to change seats on the bus.

Thank you for sharing your wisdom, insights, and practical guidance in your column. You are truly *mechazek es harabim*.

**Thank you** for your kind words and your excellent questions on a most important topic.

No, you are not overreacting. The possibility of abuse always needs to be considered. As Shlomo HaMelech taught, "Fortunate is the man who is always fearful" (*Mishlei* 28:14). While most commentaries explain that this *pasuk* refers to fear of sin, the *Metzudas Dovid* gives a more general interpretation: ". . . who is always fearful of frightening things and [consequently] protects himself from them." So according to the *Metzudas Dovid*, this *pasuk* is teaching us that it is only by being constantly vigilant that we can insure our safety and the safety of our loved ones.

The "red flag circumstance," as you put it, that parents should use as a possible indicator of abuse, however, is a *sudden* change in a child's mood or behavior. A normally outgoing and confident child, for example, who turns into a shy, withdrawn child seemingly overnight is one who should be suspected of having been victimized.

In the letter to which I was responding, the mother wrote that her child, "had a difficult time getting adjusted" to the school bus "when she began Pre 1-A." In addition, this child also "*kvetched* a little occasionally" about the school bus even after getting used to it. Finally, the mother described her daughter as, "always [having] been somewhat on the fearful side, resisting doctor visits, avoiding change, declining sleep-over invitations from friends, etc." For all of those reasons, therefore, the anxiety regarding getting on the bus this year did not sound to me like a sudden behavioral change suggesting possible abuse.

Nevertheless, since abuse is such a serious problem, it should never be dismissed too quickly. My answer to that mother, therefore, was incomplete and should have included a recommendation to investigate the bus arrangements, as you pointed out. In addition, I should have offered the following advice to her regarding the questioning of her daughter.

The mother wrote that, "We have asked her why she is so much more fearful of the school bus now than she was last year and the year before. But each time we ask, the answer is always the same: 'I don't know.'"

Children who are being abused will often fail to mention it even when asked directly, "What's wrong?" "What's the matter?" and "Why are you afraid?" In order to be assured that their children are not being abused, parents need to ask more pointed questions such as, "Is anyone doing anything to you to hurt you, frighten you, or make you feel uncomfortable?"

I know of one young man, for example, who was abused at sleepaway camp by his counselor when he was 8 years old. Whenever he spoke to his parents during that summer, however, he complained only about feeling homesick because he was not mature enough to realize that the counselor's behavior was inappropriate. Had his parents asked the question posed above, it would have increased the chances of their son disclosing the abuse about which the parents have still never learned.

I must take issue, however, with one point you made regarding the incident witnessed by your niece. You wrote that, "It's a miracle that one little girl had the courage to open up to her mother."

It is wonderful that one girl spoke to her mother about what was transpiring on the bus. I do not believe, however, that it was a miracle. Rather, it was a testimony to the open communication and warm, trusting relationship that mother had established with her daughter. Such relationships are not formed by supernatural forces but by the diligent, long-term efforts of parents who devote quality time to their children.

As Harav Shlomo Wolbe, *ztz"l*, notes in his parenting classic, *Z'riah U'binyan B'chinuch* (Feldheim, 1995, p. 16), years later, parents reap the fruits of their having cultivated warm relationships with their children when they were younger. And open communication is one of the most prized fruits in the basket.

When parents repeatedly demonstrate to their children that they are interested in any and all aspects of the children's lives, that there is no subject the children cannot discuss with them, and that regardless of the topic, the parents will listen with empathy, without undo criticism, then their children will *naturally* have the courage to report abuse to their parents.

How Can We Minimize the Rivalry Between Our 12½-Year-Old Fraternal Twins When the Boy Becomes Bar Mitzvah?

Our two oldest children are twins, age 12½. They are fraternal twins, differing in both personalities and gender. The boy is studious, hard working, and somewhat shy. The girl is more outgoing, social, and less conscientious about her schoolwork.

Even though they are different genders, they are both quite competitive with each other. They tend to quarrel often. And they each complain that we show favoritism to the other one.

What concerns us now is the boy's upcoming *bar mitzvah*. We are not planning a lavish affair, by any means. Nevertheless, there will be a *kiddush* on Shabbos and a modest *seudah* on the night of his *bar mitzvah*. Out-of-town relatives will be coming for one or both events. And we do anticipate that he will receive a fair amount of presents from many of the guests.

All of this fuss over our son will only serve to fan the fires of our daughter's jealousy. As we are a more *"yeshivishe"* family, we did not make much of a fuss over her 12th birthday and there was no *bas mitzvah* party.

So far, our daughter has not complained about any of this. We do anticipate, however, that as we get closer to the celebrations for the *bar mitzvah*, our daughter will object to the unfairness of it all and we are not sure how to handle that.

Do you have any suggestions for us?

You are right to be concerned about the sibling rivalry between your twins. Parents do have a responsibility to make sure they are not doing anything which could exacerbate that conflict. As *Chazal* have taught, "A person should never [treat] one son differently from his other children because as a result of the two *selah*s weight of silk which Yaakov Avinu added to Yosef above [that received by] his brothers (i.e., for the cloak of many colors) his brothers became jealous of him and it led to our forefathers descending [into exile and then slavery] in *Mitzrayim*" (*Shabbos* 10b, *Megillah* 16b).

Certainly, the spiritual levels of Yaakov *Avinu* and his children are beyond our limited comprehension. And when the words of *Chazal* seem to criticize them, they refer to minuscule character flaws in otherwise exemplary *tzaddikim*. Nevertheless, if *Chazal* have chosen to mention these shortcomings, it is meant for us to learn from them to improve our own behavior. And one of the lessons we must learn is to be careful not to do anything that could intensify competition between siblings.

As parents, however, you cannot resolve this problem by denying your son the celebration of his *bar mitzvah*. What you described is most likely what most or all of his classmates will have. And you do not want him to feel cheated or deprived of what would be considered normal *bar mitzvah* festivities.

On the other hand, given the history of their relationship thus far, it is reasonable to assume that your daughter may very well complain about the unfairness of her brother getting all of the limelight when they both turn 13.

In order to minimize this potential crisis, therefore, I have two suggestions for you.

First, do everything you can to make your daughter feel that she is a major player at these upcoming celebrations. Even though she does not have the leading role, she should be made to feel that she is not completely off the stage.

For example, you should play up the selection and purchase of her new dress(es) for these happy occasions. Let her feel that, as the sister of the *bar mitzvah* boy, she must also look her best. In addition, encourage her to invite a few friends to the Shabbos *kiddush* and, if possible, to the *seudah*, as well. Even one close friend at the *seudah* can make her anticipate and enjoy the event on a much more personal level.

While fraternal twins are exactly the same age, other siblings who are close in age can experience similar rivalry. This strategy of highlighting each child's unique opportunities, therefore, is one which can and should be used by all parents.

The second and much more challenging task is to prepare to answer her possible charges of "unfairness." Hopefully, she will not complain about this. But if she does, you need to be prepared, just as all parents need to know how to respond to complaints of not being "fair."

You should begin by explaining to your daughter that "fair" is not synonymous with "equal." Just because all children are not treated equally does not mean that the parents are being unfair. This, by the way, is a concept which all children must be taught, regardless of whether or not they are twins.

You can illustrate this point with a few concrete examples. For instance, just because one child has fever does not mean that all children must take antibiotics. Just because one child is full does not mean that other children cannot have seconds. And just because one child outgrew his or her coat does not mean that all children must now get new coats.

It is always helpful at this point if you can cite an example which will have personal meaning for the child you are addressing. In your case, for example, you might remind your daughter of a day this winter when her school was closed but her brother's yeshivah remained open. Should she have been sent to school simply because her brother did not have the day off? Or, was it "fair" that she had a snow day even though her brother had to go to learn?

Furthermore, you could point out to your daughter that much more time, attention, and money are spent on the gown, jewelry, and *sheva berachos* outfits that a *kallah* wears as opposed to those of the *chassan*. Since her brother will wear the same suit and hat for his *aufruf, chasunah*, and *sheva berachos* when he gets married, does that mean that her wardrobe should be similarly limited?

The bottom line of this discussion is that each child, at times, receives that which his or her siblings do not. This differential is not based on prejudice or preference. Rather, it is based on need and circumstances.

Children who learn this lesson can and will grow up to *fargin* their friends and neighbors things and opportunities that they may not have. On the other hand, children who do not learn this valuable lesson in life grow up to become adults who are jealous of their neighbors.

"*Lo sachmod*" is the last of the *Aseres Hadibros* (*Shemos* 20:14). On that *pasuk*, the *Ibn Ezra* asks, "How is it possible for someone not to desire something which is pleasing and attractive?" He answers with the following *mashal*.

If a common villager sees the king's beautiful daughter, he will not yearn to marry her because he knows that such a match is completely preposterous. From his early childhood, he has learned that the princess would be totally off limits to him. Similarly, wrote the *Ibn Ezra*, an intelligent person realizes that he is entitled to receive only that which Hashem has bestowed upon him and therefore will not covet that which belongs to someone else.

In addition, you can remind your daughter that your son's *bar mitzvah* celebrates his coming of age, something which she, as a girl, reached a year earlier. The reason for this disparity is because women mature faster and sooner than men.

Finally, if your daughter yearns for equal time in the limelight, that could present a good opening for you to discuss with her your views on the meaning of "*kol kevudah bas melech p'nimah*, All honor for the princess is inside" (*Tehillim* 45:14).

So if your daughter does complain about the unfairness of her brother's *bar mitzvah* celebrations, it will provide a valuable opportunity for you to teach her these important Torah lessons for life.

Our 7- and 9-Year-Old Boys Disrupt Our Shabbos Table With Their Sibling Rivalry

I realize that sibling rivalry is a fact of life. But sometimes, at our home, it just seems to go over the top. And then I find myself overwhelmed and exasperated.

We have, *bli ayin hara*, four children: two boys, ages 7 and 9, and two girls, ages 4 and 12. While they all get into disagreements, at times, it is the two boys who really present the greatest challenge. Not only do they quarrel 24/7 with each other, but they also attack me and my husband, accusing us of taking sides unfairly. My husband and I go out of our way to treat them the same. But no matter what we do, they are never satisfied and blame us for showing favoritism to the other.

Let me cite one example which is particularly frustrating. At the Shabbos table, whenever I serve dessert, I am always accused of giving the larger portion of cake, ice cream or whatever, to the other brother. And no matter how carefully I measure the servings, the dessert course typically triggers an avalanche of hurt and angry feelings.

We even tried inviting guests, hoping our boys would be too embarrassed to act up in front of strangers. But that did not help at all. And it was only me and my husband who ended up ashamed of our boys' misbehavior.

What can we do to bring a little peace and sanity into our home, especially around the Shabbos table?

You are correct. Sibling rivalry is a fact of life. The unique circumstances of each family, however, can serve to minimize or exacerbate the dynamics of this universal family conflict. More specifically, the age, birth order, and gender of children play a large role in determining how intense the sibling rivalry will be in any given family.

In your family, for example, the fact that your daughters are eight years apart means that there will be less feelings of competition between them. And the fact that your sons are so close in age almost guarantees that their struggles will be more intense. While there certainly are many exceptions, the general rule, therefore, is that sibling rivalry is more intense between siblings of the same gender who are closest in age.

While you and your husband may not be at all responsible for having caused the intense competition between your sons, you are nonetheless justified in searching for ways to diffuse the fireworks in your home. You may never succeed in eliminating jealousy between your two boys. But you certainly must do whatever you can to reduce the intensity of their strife.

So what can you do to tone down the volume of rivalry between your sons, especially at the Shabbos table?

One approach that has brought sanity back into many homes is to completely remove yourselves from the responsibility of calibrating the milligrams of each portion of dessert or any other treat. Instead, you place this responsibility on your children's shoulders. This will serve the all-important function of getting you and your husband out from that no-win position of being caught between your dueling duo.

Here's how you apply this strategy to the dessert course of the Shabbos *seudah*. This becomes a two-step process of portioning and selecting. The first step is measuring the portions. Before Shabbos, one son is chosen by a coin toss, card draw or any other random selection. This son is then invited into the kitchen to cut two pieces of cake of equal size or scoop out two identical bowls of ice cream. He should be given as much time as he needs to complete the process. Of course, he could also cut all of the portions. But since he may take a long time to insure that they are of equal size, as a practical matter, it will save time if he only cuts two.

Once the two dessert portions have been equalized by one son, the second step is to allow the *other* son to pick whichever portion he wants. And then next week, or next meal, the order is reversed. The child who picked first must slice the pie. And the child who measured the portions now gets to choose first.

This method will not prevent your sons from taunting each other with, "Ha, ha! I got the bigger piece this time!" That is unavoidable. But it will at least relieve you of the accusations of unfairness because you did not cut the cake nor did you decide which son gets which piece.

Of course, not all unfairness charges are as easily managed as the dessert dilemma you presented. Sometimes, for example, there are real and unavoidable incidents of inequality which no family can escape.

I recall, for example, when my older brother became a *bar mitzvah,* a family friend came to the celebration with a modest, conventional gift. Two and a half years later, when I became a *bar mitzvah,* this same family friend presented me with an electronic gift that raised eyebrows throughout my family.

Was that fair? Certainly not. My parents, *a"h,* however, explained to both of us that this friend's business had boomed during the previous year and he had a lot more disposable income than two and a half years earlier. Some things in life, they told us, simply cannot be equalized. In all candor, however, I must admit that as the recipient of the larger *bar mitzvah* gift, I found it much easier to accept that lesson than my brother.

Finally, not every incident of sibling bickering can or needs to be eliminated. Children learn priceless social skills of conflict resolution by crossing swords with their brothers and sisters. These skills learned at home as children will stand them in good stead throughout their lives as adults. In marriage, for example, and at work, their relationships will be enhanced by these priceless skills they learned, practiced, and sharpened when they were squabbling with their siblings as children.

Our 10-Year-Old Son
Wants To Go To Sleepaway Camp
But We Suspect He Will Be Homesick

We have three children, a 10-year-old boy and two girls, 6 and 12.

Three years ago, our oldest went to sleepaway camp for half the summer and loved every minute. When she came home, she begged us to send her for the whole summer the next year, which we did. And she is now very eagerly looking forward to her fourth summer at the same camp.

Two years ago when we came to visit our daughter at camp, our son made it very clear to us that he would "never" want to go to sleepaway camp. Last year he repeated his comment, adding that he could not even understand why his oldest sister was so happy about attending an overnight camp.

We understand that each child is different and we never made an issue of it one way or the other. We supported our older daughter's choice with the same nonjudgmental attitude with which we supported our son's decision to attend day camp. As he has had a few minor episodes of homesickness in the past, we understood that he was simply not ready to be away from home for so long.

This year, however, almost his entire class is planning to attend the same overnight camp. And our son has now completely changed his tune. He even denies any mixed feelings about camp and is begging us to register him before it is too late.

We are reluctant to register him, however, because we are afraid that he is not being honest with himself. We feel that he may only be responding to peer pressure. And we are concerned that he will become homesick once he gets to camp. Of course, we would certainly let him come home if he wanted to, but we would prefer that he avoid the discomfort and embarrassment that would undoubtedly cause.

On the other hand, we would not want to hold him back from doing what all of his classmates are doing this summer. Without close friends at day camp, he will not enjoy the experience nearly as much as he has in the past.

Based on the background we have presented, which of these two choices do you feel would be the best for our son?

Adam HaRishon and Chavah were the only people in the history of the world who did not have parents. Even so, when they married, the Torah tells us, "Therefore a man should separate from his father and mother and cling to his wife" (*Bereishis* 2:24). This *pasuk*, which Rashi informs us was uttered by *ruach hakodesh*, could not be referring to Adam. It must, consequently, be directed at all future generations. And the separation alluded to must be seen as a gradual developmental process, rather than an event at one moment in time.

Harav Moshe Meir Weiss, *shlita*, Rav of the Agudas Yisrael of Staten Island, once asked, why does the *pasuk* begin, "Therefore?" He explained that the previous *pasuk* quotes Adam HaRishon declaring upon meeting Chavah, "This time [she is] a bone from my bones and flesh of my flesh." The unique bond between Adam and Chavah would never be recreated again throughout history. *Therefore, ruach hakodesh* declares, in order to solidify the husband/wife relationship, it will be necessary for all *other* people to separate from their parents in order to have successful marriages.

As children grow and mature, they gradually learn to tolerate longer and longer separations from their parents. For infants, mother stepping into the next room triggers tears of fright and panic. After high school, the relative independence of dormitory life in yeshivah or seminary may even appear attractive and desirable. In between, there are smaller but no-less-significant separation milestones of attending school and, later, overnight camp. In order for children to succeed in making the transition from childhood dependence to adult independence and marriage, therefore, it is necessary for them to master all of the developmental steps along the way. And attending sleepaway camp is one of those critical steps.

You are using excellent judgment, therefore, in not wanting to hold your son back from attending sleepaway camp this summer. Especially since so many of his classmates are going this year, it would be a major blow to his self-esteem if he were not allowed to join them.

Your concerns about him becoming homesick, however, are quite justified. The greatest predictor of future behavior is past performance. Since he has had "episodes of homesickness" before, you are correct in assuming that he would be a likely candidate for experiencing homesickness at camp this summer.

The mistake you are making here, however, is assuming that you have only two alternatives: Send him to camp and subject him to the disgrace of homesickness or protect him from homesickness by sending him to day camp. There is a third choice. And that is to register him for sleepaway camp and then work with him from now until the summer to inoculate him against homesickness.

While no one can offer you a guarantee, it is highly likely that if you adopt the following plan, your son will be sufficiently prepared for sleepaway camp that he will suffer little, if any, homesickness.

√ Discuss the upcoming separation. Do not allow your son to pretend that everything will be fine without planning ahead or that talking about it will make it worse. Asking him to project himself into the future is an important first step toward minimizing his anxiety surrounding the separation. Emphasize the positive by telling him that you expect that he will have a good time at camp. Nevertheless, proper preparation is the greatest safeguard against the possibility of unmanageable anxiety due to homesickness.

√ Ask him what he anticipates will be the hardest part for him. Then discuss with him strategies he can use to calm and/or soothe himself if and when he experiences the first pangs of homesickness. For example, he can think about his favorite activities at camp. He can remind himself that feelings of homesickness are normal and will pass in time. Or, he can tell himself that he will see you soon on visiting day which is really not that far off. Ask him what, if anything, helped in the past. And help him adapt those tactics to the camping experience.

√ Encourage your son to spend the night with a friend or relative as a practice separation. For example, he could spend Shabbos with his grandparents or an aunt and uncle. Or, he could invite a classmate to sleep over and then accept the friend's offer to reciprocate.

√ When he comes home from the overnight stay, be sure to ask him how it went. Did he feel the slightest bit homesick? If so, when and how did he cope with it? What did he tell himself? What strategies did he learn which could be applied to the longer separation this summer?

√ Review his homesickness history. Go over the incidents from the past in which he felt varying degrees of homesickness. Which was the worst? Which was the easiest? And what was the reason for this difference? Does he think he would feel the same way today? If not, why? What did he learn from those episodes? Looking back over the years, does he feel he has made any progress in this area? If so, what helped? And how could he apply those tools to the upcoming summer-camp experience?

√ Prepare for the probability of some feelings of homesickness. Tell your son that these are common emotions that should not cause alarm or panic. Brainstorm together what special items he should bring along that would help him cope with such feelings. For example, I have often recommended that parents write a special "homesickness letter" or record a "homesickness tape" which the child should save for "emergencies" only. Just having such back-up plans can be very reassuring for an anxious child.

√ Finally, discuss with your son what the frequency of communication will be. It is important for him to know, in advance, whether you will or will not be calling him. Try to strike a balance between being available but not hovering over him. And try to take cues from him once he gets to camp. For example, don't ask him if he's homesick, but discuss it with him if he brings it up when on the phone with you.

Our 7-Year-Old Son Seems Obsessed With His 5-Year-Old Sister

We always enjoy reading your column and find your advice very practical.

We have five children, *ka"h*, between the ages of 8 and 1 ¹/₂. All of them are girls except our second child, age 7.

The relationships between them seem to be normal with the usual sibling rivalry — but not beyond. This is all true except for the relationship between our seven-year-old son and his next-in-line sister, age 5 (almost 6). He seems to be overly preoccupied with her and is constantly putting her down verbally and even hitting her. On the occasional times when they do get along, their games tend to be very wild.

He is not like this with any of his other siblings, with whom he plays very nicely. In every other way, he plays nicely and is a very responsible and sensitive child.

Please advise us regarding how to deal with this. We find that the more we tell him to leave her alone, the more he is at her. We're at our wits' end! Thank you very much, in advance.

The wild play you observe, at times, between your son and his next youngest sister is an excellent illustration of the very healthy phenomenon called sublimation. What is sublimation?

Children, like adults, experience a wide range of emotions. These can be classified into two basic categories: positive and negative. Positive emotions are the feelings we enjoy and make us feel good, such as affection, appreciation, pride, happiness, and love. Negative emotions are the feelings we do not like and try to avoid, such as annoyance, irritation, anger, jealousy, sadness, and hate.

Daily living and interactions with others trigger a wide range of both positive and negative emotions. We cannot choose to experience only positive feelings. Whether we like it or not, therefore, we must deal with negative emotions on a regular basis.

Whenever we experience negative emotions, such as anger, we often feel the urge to act in a manner that is improper. For example, we might feel like breaking something. *Chazal* have taught, however, that, "Whoever rends his garment in anger or breaks his vessels in anger or discards his money in anger should be considered as one who worships idols" (*Shabbos* 105b).

If, on the other hand, one channels these negative emotions into acceptable behavior, the feelings are discharged without negative consequences. That is referred to as sublimation. For example, one might channel these feelings into the performance of a *mitzvah* such as *kri'ah*.

Regarding the *mitzvah* of *kri'ah*, Harav Shimshon Rephael Hirsch, *ztz"l*, wrote, "As the immediate first expression of grief, *kri'ah*, i.e. rending of one's garment, has been instituted" (*Horeb* p. 209). Furthermore, the Rambam wrote, "The purpose of the *mitzvah* of *kri'ah* is that through it he [the *aveil*] cools off and his emotions are settled" (Commentary on *Mishnayos, Shabbos* Ch. 13).

Coming back to your children, the rough play you described represents a healthy sublimation of your son's jealous, competitive and even resentful feelings toward his sister. By discharging his emotions in this more acceptable fashion, it enables him — at least temporarily — to restrain himself from verbally or physically attacking her. Your role here is to understand how important this unruly play is in helping your son deal with his intense feelings of sibling rivalry.

When they do not get along, apparently the majority of the time, you must understand that your son feels very threatened by his next youngest sister. The 8-year-old is older, and presumably larger, than he is. She is, therefore, in a completely separate category. The 1 1/2-year-old is a baby and, therefore, not much of threat to his standing in the pecking order. That leaves the 5-year-old and the one under her. As the 5-year-old is the closest in age to your son, he has targeted her as his primary nemesis.

When you "tell him to leave her alone," you naturally assume that you are being a good parent by protecting your daughter from her bullying big brother. You are obviously unaware as to why your protecting her should provoke him to increase his attacks. I will explain that to you, therefore, so that you can recognize how you are actually planting the seeds for his next assault every time you rally to her defense.

All children who have siblings are universally plagued by doubts regarding which child is more favored in the eyes of their parents. Since parents wield the power to withhold or dispense attention, affection, and privileges, getting on a parent's good side and jockeying for more advantageous positions become obsessive preoccupations of all children.

If a conflict breaks out — which it always does — between any two siblings, the response of the parents becomes absolutely critical. If the parents will side with, defend or justify either child, then the other child will take that as a sign that he or she is now in a weaker, more vulnerable, and more insecure position in the family.

This will automatically trigger two reactions in the child who was scolded. First, it will provoke intense feelings of resentment toward the sibling who was favored by the parental intervention. If not for him/her, the child thinks to himself/herself, I would not be receiving this unpleasant rebuke from my parents. (S)he is all that stands in the way of my having a warm, close and loving relationship with my parents. If only (s)he were out of the picture, then everything would be blissful.

The second reaction set off in the child who was reprimanded for attacking a sibling is that this child will now feel more insecure. Do my parents still love me, (s)he asks herself/himself. In order to reassure herself/himself, therefore, (s)he must set up a test in which the parents will be forced to choose between the same two children. If my parents side with me, (s)he thinks to herself/himself, then I'm not as spurned as I thought. The child then seeks another opportunity to attack her/his sibling. And so the vicious cycle continues and intensifies exactly as you described.

The solution to all of this is to avoid arbitrating sibling conflicts as much as possible. Often a disclaimer of, "I'm sorry. I didn't see what just happened," is sufficient. Once you refuse to accept your children's testimony as if it were concrete evidence, you can dislodge yourself from the impossible position you currently occupy between your son and daughter. Over time, if you are consistent with this approach, *shalom bayis* will eventually return to your home.

In order to give you the "other side of the story," I will disclose that I was the youngest child in my family of origin. And I can still recall how I learned to provoke my older brother's anger with a certain facial expression when we were both very young.

My parents, *a"h*, always came to my rescue whenever I was attacked by my brother. Eventually I learned that there were so many times when they were not available that relying on them was not a viable defense strategy.

In time, without the benefit of their protection, I learned to protect myself. As my brother was older and larger, I could not employ any physical means of self-defense. Instead, I was forced to hone my verbal skills. It is entirely possible, therefore, that my choice of profession resulted, at least in part, from my early training in the school of hard knocks at the university of sibling rivalry.

How Should Our Children Relate to Their Secular Relatives?

I am concerned about how our children should relate to their secular relatives. I have heard that children see the world as black and white, without any gray. Therefore, should we avoid scenarios where our children could develop a close relationship with our secular relatives and thereby be confused between a "nice person" and the correct *derech*? For example, should we only make contact with secular relatives when we have to, such as when they want to visit, or for a *simchah*, etc., thereby avoiding the possibility of developing close relationships? Also, should we go as far as not having our children getting help with their homework from such relatives, either in person or over the phone, in order to avoid this?

What you heard is absolutely correct. Children do tend to see the world in absolute terms. And the younger they are, the more this is so. As they mature, however, children learn to become increasingly more aware of the gray areas that encompass most of the world in which we live.

Unfortunately, some young people reach adulthood without mastering this vital perception. What is normal in childhood, therefore, is pathological for adults. And seeing the world in "all or nothing" terms can severely handicap any individual who suffers from such a distorted way of thinking. Three actual case examples will illustrate this point.

Menachem spent the past year in Eretz Yisrael. He learned very little and returned home with a profound sense of failure. The reason for this is that he never remained in one yeshivah for more than six weeks. As soon as he encountered a rebbi, a *bachur*, or an aspect of the accommodations with which he was dissatisfied, he left the yeshivah. In short, if a yeshivah did not have everything he wanted, he saw it as having nothing to offer.

Daniel is unhappily married. He believes that his wife is the sole cause of his pain. He is so depressed that he has even consulted with professional marriage counselors. He is still suffering today because he has not found a therapist who will categorically agree with him that he is not at fault in any way. If this therapist does not completely take my side, Daniel reasons, then I must move on and find one who will.

Shaindy is almost engaged. The young man is eager to propose but Shaindy keeps telling the shadchan that she is "not ready yet." What is holding her back? Although she acknowledges that most of her "check list" has been satisfied, there are a few minor details that are missing. These shortcomings, however, are not serious enough to break off the *shidduch*. If he had *everything* she wanted, she would not be so indecisive. Since he is not perfect, however, she feels stuck and reaches out for advice that only serves to confuse her even more.

Your job as a parent, therefore, is to make sure your children do not grow up to be Menachems, Daniels or Shaindys. Help them see gray whenever they perceive only black or white. Teach them, for example, that good people are capable of doing bad things and bad people can sometimes do good things.

Parents are definitely good people. They can, however, make honest mistakes in judgment. Acknowledging that fact goes a long way toward helping children see more gray in their world. And one of the best methods to accomplish that goal is for parents to apologize to children whenever necessary. Appropriate apologies from parents teach children to respect themselves and validate their judgment of right and wrong. In addition, it shows them that good people can make mistakes and still be good people.

Another strategy is to share with children some of the myriad examples of *Chazal* teaching us to eschew absolute categorizing of people, such as the following enlightening episode (*Sanhedrin* 102b).

Rav Ashi announced to his *talmidim* that the next day he would begin to expound on the *mishnah* that teaches that the wicked king, Menashe, has no share in *Olam Haba*. In doing so, he sarcastically referred to Menashe with the term "our friend."

That night, Menashe appeared to Rav Ashi in a dream. He asked, "Do you really consider me to be your equal? Do you know what part of the loaf one must cut first after reciting *ha'motzi*?"

Rav Ashi confessed that he did not know.

Menashe then replied, "You do not even know from where to cut the bread after reciting *ha'motzi* and you still consider me your equal?"

Rav Ashi asked Menashe to teach him the answer, promising to give over that *halachah* the next day in the *beis midrash* in Menashe's name.

Menashe replied that one should cut the part of the loaf that is baked first (meaning the place with the thickest crust).

"If you are so wise," asked Rav Ashi, "why did you chase after idolatry [when you were alive]?"

"Had you been there," Menashe responded, "you would have picked up the end of your cloak to run more quickly as a result of the urge to worship idols that was prevalent then."

Returning to your dilemma, suppose children were told that only *frum* people are good and all non*frum* people are bad. That might sound like an effective strategy to ensure the children's adherence to a Torah way of life.

Let us consider, however, what the long-term consequences could be. How would that child react when he or she encounters the first *frum* person who does not behave properly? (And regrettably, we must admit that this is possible.) The entire house of cards would collapse, creating a major crisis of faith. If, however, a child is raised to understand that non*frum* people can still be good but a *frum* lifestyle is even more desirable, then a crisis of faith is much less likely.

I do not believe it is harmful, therefore, for a child to have close relationships with secular relatives. Two words of caution are in order here. First, as in all other areas of *chinuch*, before implementing any plan, you should first be consulting with *daas* Torah. Secondly, the parents must closely monitor those relationships, to make sure that the secular relatives are not challenging or undermining the child's Torah *chinuch* in any way.

If these relatives, for example, are attempting to "enlighten" the child by encouraging him to adopt their secular lifestyle, then the parents must impose whatever limits are necessary to protect the child from this potentially harmful influence.

Ideally, you should try to arrange for your children to interact with their not-yet-*frum* relatives in your home. By inviting them into your home for

Shabbos or *Yom Tov*, for example, you can insure that your relatives will be influenced by your Torah lifestyle and not the other way around.

Finally, it is very important that you not send your children a mixed or confusing message. You cannot, for example, allow them to interact with their secular relatives and then grill them on the details of the conversation. You must, therefore, feel comfortable with the parameters that you set. Just as you cannot give children permission to drive the family car and then follow closely behind in a second vehicle, so too, you should not allow your children to interact with their relatives and then hover over them like a mother bird.

Therefore, if you feel you cannot trust your children and/or your non-*frum* relatives, then do not do so. But do not act trusting if you are too uncomfortable because the discomfort will show through and greatly confuse your children.

What I have offered you are general guidelines. Since you did not indicate the ages of your children, I could not be more specific. It should be stressed, however, that the age of the child does make a difference when it comes to exposing your children to potentially negative influences. Younger children, for example, usually require closer supervision, while older children can be trusted with more freedom and autonomy. The individual personality of each child should also be taken into consideration. Some children are, by nature, more gullible or easily influenced. Others are more cautious and street smart. In each case, therefore, as with so many other matters, parents need to know the needs and natures of each child in order to make the most informed and appropriate parenting decisions.

My 8-Year-Old Son Totally Lacks Derech Eretz

My 8-year-old son has driven me to my wits' end. I am turning to you now as a last resort.

He is not really a major problem at school. But his English teacher and his rebbi both report that he does not have any close friends.

I am concerned about his lack of friends. He rarely invites anyone to come to our house to play. And the few invitations he receives he turns down. His social issues, however, are not the reason for this letter.

What pushed me to write is his attitude. He acts as if he is the parent and I am the child. He is demanding, uncooperative, disobedient, and, worst of all, disrespectful. He calls me names and uses language that I would not even want to put on paper. In short, he totally lacks *derech eretz*.

While he was always a difficult child, this year has been off the charts. He is the youngest of five. And I never went through anything like this with any of his older siblings.

I even consulted with a psychologist, looking for some parental guidance. My husband wasn't able to take off from work so I went myself. The psychologist gave me an appointment to bring my son in for an evaluation. When it came time for the appointment, however, my son adamantly refused to get in the car. I even tried to bribe him; but nothing worked and we ended up missing the appointment.

I don't know what else I can do. What would you recommend?

Part of the problem here is that you met with the psychologist alone. If your husband could not take time off from work, you should have looked for another therapist who would see you after your husband finishes work or on the weekend.

By going alone to the psychologist, you sent the wrong messages to your family. First, you were confirming for your husband that this is more your responsibility than his. And that is simply not so. As *Chazal* have taught, "There are three partners in [the creation of] man: *HaKadosh Baruch Hu*, his father, and his mother" (*Kiddushin* 30b). While the latter two partners are not equal to the first, they should be equal to each other.

Secondly, if your son learns that only you met with the psychologist, that tells him that the whole business of going for the evaluation is not something that Mommy and Tatty are supporting equally. In order for any parenting project to succeed, therefore, it must have the complete backing of both parents.

Does that mean that if one parent is opposed to or declines to endorse the evaluation that it must be ruled out? No, not at all. But it does mean you are fighting an uphill battle whenever you arrange for an evaluation without the full endorsement and participation of both parents.

In your letter, you did not mention how you presented the idea of the evaluation to your son. The wording of that explanation is quite significant. Sometimes parents say, "We don't know what to do with you. So we are taking you to someone who will tell us what we can do to get you to behave." When presented like that, an evaluation sounds to a child like a punishment.

Other parents say, "We want you to talk to someone who will help you to be less angry." When presented that way, the evaluation sounds like an attempt to fix the child. And children are almost as reluctant to get fixed as adults are.

For maximum results, parents should say, "We have noticed that you are not as happy as we would like you to be. We have consulted with someone who could help us to be better parents. He said he could work with us but would need to meet with you first." While that is true, it also reassures the child that he has nothing to lose and a lot to gain by participating in the process.

Now to your question. If your son resists the evaluation, he should not be forced. That does not preclude your going back to the psychologist for parental guidance. Even without seeing your child, the psychologist can discuss with you the details of what is going on at home and then offer practical suggestions. Sometimes, as the following case example will illustrate, the child's refusal to meet with a therapist represents his or her unconscious message to the therapist, "My parent needs more help than I do." As a general rule, therefore, if children who need professional help refuse to go, it is highly recommended for the parents to go themselves, without the child, to get advice and tools that will help them deal with that child.

Some time ago, for example, a mother consulted with me regarding her 7-year-old son who was behaving quite similarly to your son. Her husband "did not believe in psychology," so she came without him.

When it came time for the evaluation, the woman arrived with her son who threw a tantrum in my waiting room and refused to speak with me. Even when his mother offered to come in with him, he still insisted and then demanded that she take him home. He was completely unwilling to even look at the toys and games I utilized to try to engage him. After 15 minutes of this standoff, the woman finally relented and took her son home.

"What do I do now?" she asked over the phone later that day.

"Perhaps you and I should have a talk," I suggested.

She agreed and made an appointment for herself. When she came in, we talked a little about her son. Then I asked her to tell me about her marriage. She opened up and confided to me that her husband was emotionally abusive to her. He was controlling, demanding, and often insulting. For example, she came home one day and found some of her clothing missing from her drawers. Her husband matter-of-factly explained that he had discarded those items because he "did not like them."

Chazal have taught, "This is what people say, 'Comments that a child makes in public [he heard] either from his father or his mother [in private]'" (*Succah* 56b). With that in mind, I pointed out to this woman that her son's treatment of her sounded quite similar to the way her husband was behaving toward her.

She immediately saw the connection that — hard as it is to believe — had eluded her until I mentioned it. She then asked me what she could do about it.

"I think you know what you have to do," I replied.

"Do you mean that I have to learn to stand up for myself?"

"Exactly! But perhaps you should begin with your youngest child and then work your way up."

Instead of my telling her how to assert herself, I recommended that she try to trust her own judgment and report back to me the following week. Over the next few weeks, she made dramatic progress in restoring her parental authority with her children. Her older children were somewhat taken aback by her new approach to dealing with them. I recommended that she meet with each one separately and give them the following explanation. "I've let too much go for too long. From now on, I expect you to . . ."

Although her husband never consented to enter marital counseling, he did ease up on her somewhat as she continued to build her confidence. And we ended our work shortly after she registered for a computer course, launching a new career for herself.

Am I Too Lenient Or Is My Wife Too Strict?

Perhaps you can help me and my wife resolve an ongoing dispute we have regarding how we should be dealing with our children. And what happened last Sunday is a good illustration of our disagreement.

Our oldest child, a boy age 12, went out in the morning after breakfast to play with his friends. As he has no day camp on Sundays, he really had no responsibilities at all that day. Well before it grew dark, he came home.

My wife was very upset that our son had not come home or even called at all during the day. Although she knew he had gone to play with friends, she had no idea exactly where he was or when he would be coming home. She felt that he had behaved irresponsibly. And she wanted me to take him to task for that.

I, on the other hand, do not feel our son did anything wrong. He did tell his mother he was going out before he left. And he even informed her which friends he was planning to meet. He is a mature boy and has never given us any reason to question his judgment. And had my wife asked him to call during the day, he most certainly would have complied with her wishes.

My question, therefore, is: Am I too laid back and lenient, as my wife contends, or is she too strict and rigid, as I feel she is?

**While I may not resolve** your dispute with each other, I may be able to shed some light on areas in which you both may need some improvement in your respective approaches to parenting.

As far as your wife's position is concerned, it is unfair to require children of any age to fulfill parental expectations that have not been clearly articulated. Regardless of how reasonable it is to hear from your son at some time during the day, if you have not informed him of this requirement, you cannot hold him accountable for failing to comply. Your son, after all, should never be expected to read your mind in order to know what you want from him.

Whenever parents do communicate their behavioral expectations to their children, however, they must be sure to do so in a very clear, concrete, and unambiguous manner. Phrases such as "soon" or "on time" should be avoided. Instead, parents should say, "within the next two hours," or, "before 6 o'clock." Parents must speak to children, as the saying goes, "Rochel, *bitcha ha'k'tanah* (Rochel, your daughter, the younger one)," a reference to Yaakov Avinu's specificity in speaking with his deceitful future father-in-law, Lavan. (See *Bereishis* 29:18 and Rashi's commentary on that *pasuk*.)

Regarding your own parenting style, you must learn to appreciate the value of setting limits for children.

Unfortunately, today, many parents believe that they are doing a disservice to their children by setting limits. They believe that loving children means satisfying their wishes all the time.

Of course, nothing could be further from the truth. Imposing proper limitations is an act of love. And when parents fail to set limits for their children, they emotionally cripple them for life.

Examples abound today of the devastating consequences of overindulgent parenting. We see many dysfunctional adults whose current difficulties in life can be traced back to their unstructured childhoods growing up in homes where there were no restrictions.

The following are but a few illustrations.

- ✓ Those who are so incapable of controlling their impulses that they have fallen hopelessly in debt by having maxed out on their credit cards and now can barely make the minimum payments each month;

- ✓ Those who feel such an exaggerated sense of entitlement that they truly believe they are above the law and will not get caught if they speed, drive under the influence or commit "white-collar" crimes;
- ✓ Those who are so accustomed to having decisions made for them that they are paralyzed by indecision and fear of commitment when confronted by choices of clothing, jobs, and/or marital prospects.
- ✓ Those who are so used to having things their way that they alienate coworkers, friends, and spouses by their rigid unwillingness to cooperate, collaborate, and compromise;
- ✓ Those whose expectations for gratification are so unrealistic that they have practically lost their ability to feel and express appropriate appreciation to others.

In Scripture we are told the tragic story of Adoniyahu, the elder son of Dovid HaMelech, whose unsuccessful attempt to usurp the throne ultimately led to his execution. There it records that Dovid HaMelech never reprimanded his son for anything (*I Melachim* 1:6). Commenting on that *pasuk*, Rashi noted, "This comes to teach that whoever holds back reproof from his child will contribute to that child's premature death."

We all want our children to grow into independent, successful, and contented adults. In order to help them reach those goals, we must not abdicate our responsibility to set appropriate limits for them as they mature. This will enable them to learn self-control, build frustration tolerance, develop self-reliance, respect the needs and feelings of others, and appropriately postpone gratification.

With regard to your son, he certainly did nothing wrong this past Sunday. You and your wife, however, failed to be *mechaneich* him properly. To allow a 12-year-old boy to have a full day with "no responsibilities at all" is to abdicate your duties as parents.

Children most definitely need free time on the weekend in order to relax and recharge for the coming week, as we all do. But they also need limits set for them by their parents. For example, you or your wife could have asked him to fit in a brief defined period of learning and/or household chores at a convenient time somewhere in his long, camp-free Sunday. This need not restrict his freedom or his social life. But it will add the vital nutrient of limits which *Chazal* identified as sorely missing from Adoniyahu's diet.

Was I Wrong to Bring Our 10-Year-Old Daughter to Her Grandfather's Levayah?

Last week my father-in-law, *z"l*, was *niftar*. Our 10-year-old daughter asked if she could attend the *levayah* and my husband and I didn't know what to do.

On the one hand, our daughter was very close to her *zaidie* whom she would visit at least once a week. As we live only three short blocks from his home, she would often walk over by herself just to say hello.

Two months prior to his *petirah*, my father-in-law, *z"l*, was hospitalized. From then on, she had no contact with him, even though she repeatedly asked to visit him, because the hospital did not allow children onto his floor and he was too weak to speak on the phone. So, it seemed only right to allow her to come.

On the other hand, she had never attended a *levayah* before and we were not sure if she would be able to handle it. We had no one to ask about this and had to decide quickly. With much ambivalence, in the end, we decided to let her attend.

Three days later, when I was in my father-in-law's kitchen preparing lunch for the *aveilim*, one of my sisters-in-law came in and scolded me for having brought our daughter to the *levayah*. "Children have no place at a *levayah*," she said. "You should have known better. This could have been traumatic for her. That was an irresponsible thing for you to do."

Now I'm not sure we made the correct decision. Even though our daughter seems to have dealt with the whole thing quite well, I would very much like to hear your views on bringing children to a *levayah*. Do you agree with my sister-in-law that we acted irresponsibly? What would you have recommended if we had consulted with you?

Avraham Avinu and Sarah Imeinu were married for decades without having any children. When Avraham Avinu was 99 years old, he performed a *bris milah* on himself without any anesthesia. Then, the following year, when he was 100 years old and Sarah Imeinu was ninety, she gave birth to Yitzchak Avinu.

Could there be any more miraculous birth than that? Is there any more evidence needed that such a supernatural event was decreed by Heaven? Yet, in spite of all of that, there were people who tried to ridicule our first Matriarch. Rashi refers to those people as *"leitzanei hador"* (*Bereishis* 25:19).

Why is it necessary for us to know how the *leitzanei hador* were trying to disparage Sarah Imeinu? Perhaps it was to provide *chizuk* for all future generations. If someone on the elevated stature of Sarah Imeinu had to endure derision after the miraculous birth of Yitzchak Avinu, then we should not be astonished if we are also mocked whenever we pursue any appropriate course of action.

This does not mean to say that I am labeling your sister-in-law as a *leitz, chas v'shalom*. But I am trying to point out not only that I believe you acted correctly, but also that you should not let someone else's unjustified criticism undermine your confidence in your own judgment.

For the sake of others who may find themselves, *chas v'shalom*, in a similar predicament, let me share the following guidelines I used to arrive at my assessment of your decision.

All children do not have the same level of maturity. Ask any elementary school teacher or rebbi and they will confirm this fact of life. Some children are immature, acting more like children who are chronologically much younger. Other children, however, display an emotional maturity comparable to children much older.

When assessing whether or not a child is "old enough" for anything, the age of the child should not be the deciding factor. What is more important is the child's emotional maturity.

When it comes to deciding, therefore, whether or not to allow a child to attend a *levayah*, there can be no fixed age limits or cutoff point. The decision, then, must be based on an individualized assessment of the motivation and coping skills of that child.

Regarding the motivation, the question must always be asked, "Whose desire is it that this child should attend the *levayah*?" If relatives of the child would like the child to be present, that is not sufficient justification. The needs of the child should always supersede the wishes of any adult.

In your case, it was your daughter's wish to attend the funeral of her *zaidie*. And there appears to have been good reason for her to want to do so. As she was denied access to him during his final illness, her presence at the *levayah* could help her bring closure to the obviously fond relationship she had with this important person in her life.

The coping skills are more difficult to assess. In order to do that fully, one must take into consideration how the child has dealt with potentially stressful experiences in the past. Does this child shy away from anything which could be frightening, unpleasant or even gruesome? If so, then this child may not be ready to attend his or her first *levayah*.

If, on the other hand, this child has demonstrated an ability to maintain his or her emotional equilibrium in potentially stressful situations, then he or she may be able to handle the experience of attending a *levayah*.

In your case, the fact that your daughter asked to see her grandfather in the hospital indicates that she may not be so squeamish as to fear a hospital visit. If so, then she may have already demonstrated a higher level of maturity.

Perhaps the best method of measuring children's emotional maturity level and coping skills is to describe in detail what actually happens at a *levayah*. Do not sugarcoat it for them. And do not exaggerate it, either. Simply walk them through what they will see and what they can expect to hear. Tell them that people will be crying, some uncontrollably. Tell them how long it will take. And tell them that they may leave at any time if they feel it is too much for them.

After giving them this orientation, ask them if that is what they thought happens at a *levayah*. Do they still want to attend? If the answer is "yes," and they have managed well in the past in potentially stressful situations, then you should allow a child to attend the *levayah* of a close relative.

Returning to your original questions, I believe you acted correctly and responsibly in allowing your daughter to attend her *zaidie*'s *levayah*. And the only mistake you made was allowing your sister-in-law's misguided condemnation to undermine your trust in your own good judgment.

From your letter, there was no indication whether your sister-in-law was a daughter of the *niftar*, a daughter-in-law, or related to you from the other side of your family. If she was a daughter and therefore one of the *aveilim*, her response to you may need to be viewed in light of the pain of her loss. If she was not an *aveil* but only a daughter-in-law like yourself, I wonder how she handled the question of *levayah* attendance with her own children. Did she not allow them to attend and later regretted her decision? Was she feeling guilty and needing to attack you to make herself feel better? Perhaps she saw your decision as showing her up in some way?

Regardless of your sister-in-law's motives, you could have responded to her in a nonconfrontational manner. For example, you could have said, "I believe that parents should decide on a case-by-case basis what is in the best interest of each child. My husband and I carefully deliberated with each other and concluded that she should be allowed to attend. Had you participated in our discussion, I'm sure you would have agreed that we did act responsibly."

3 Teenagers

My 14-Year-Old Daughter Is Ungrateful

I'm afraid my daughter has become a *kafui tov* and I'm wondering what, if anything, I can do about it.

My daughter is 14 years old and in ninth grade at one of the local Bais Yaakov high schools. This year has been especially challenging for her academically. I don't think she was properly prepared in elementary school for the level of work she is required to do in high school. Even with proper preparation, however, the work load she is carrying seems to me, as a parent, to be rather excessive.

Although I am concerned that there is much too much homework assigned every night, that is not why I am writing to you. What prompted me to ask you for help was an incident that happened this week involving a major report my daughter had to write for school.

My daughter had been complaining about this particular assignment for weeks before it was due. She simply felt overwhelmed by it and did not feel she could even get started with it by herself. Last week my husband had pity on her and offered to help. He literally spent hours, which involved much *mesiras nefesh*, trying to help her with this report. In the end, he practically wrote the entire thing himself.

Throughout this process, my husband heard barely any appreciation from our daughter. Mostly, all she did was criticize him, saying things like, "Oh, you don't understand," "No, my teacher doesn't want it that way," and, "No, that's no good," etc.

I was very upset to see how unappreciative my daughter was for all the time and effort my husband put in to help her with this assignment. Generally, my daughter is polite and says her "please" and "thank-you"s at the table. But there have been times when I have chauffeured her to an errand when she left the car without thanking me for taking her.

Is there anything you feel we can or should be doing to eradicate this *middah* of *kafui tov* from our daughter?

While I have not met your daughter, from your letter she does not sound like a *"kafui tov"* to me. That is a harsh term that should be reserved for someone who is so ungrateful as to *never* acknowledge favors done for them. If your daughter "generally" expresses appreciation but sometimes fails, that would indicate that there is room for improvement in her *middos*, but not that she has earned the derogatory title of a *kafui tov*.

Hakaras hatov is an extremely important *middah* for parents to instill in their children, as it is a hallmark of our people. We are called Israelites, Hebrews, and sometimes terms which should not be printed in a family newspaper. The one term used most often, however, by others as well as ourselves, is "Jews." Where does the term "Jew" come from?

The term Jew is a derivative of Yehudah, the name of the last Kingdom of Israel and the name of the fourth son of Leah Imeinu. When Leah Imeinu chose a name for her fourth son, the Torah tells us why she chose this name. She declared, "This time, I will praise Hashem" (*Bereishis* 29:35). And on this Rashi adds, "Because I have taken more than my portion."

Leah Imeinu knew through *ruach hakodesh* that there were to be 12 tribes. As Yaakov Avinu had four wives, Leah Imeinu could therefore expect to have three sons. When she had her fourth son, she realized that she now had more than she could have expected and chose a name for her son to reflect her feelings of gratitude. So within the very term "Jew" lies the foundation of the centrality of *hakaras hatov* in *Yiddishkeit*.

It is always a good idea to give children gentle reminders to be more polite and respectful to the other parent. A father, for example, should prompt his children to say "thank you" to their mother. When parents stick up for each other in this way, children do not see this as a selfish grab for honor. Rather, they see it for what it is: teaching proper *middos*.

In your case, therefore, there would have been nothing wrong had you pointed out to your daughter that she was remiss in not showing more appreciation to her father for all the help he gave her with her report. You could have said, "Tatty really spent a lot of time with you. You could have thanked him a bit more than you did."

If you want your daughter, or any child, to improve his or her *middos*, one of the best ways to accomplish that is to set a proper example with your own behavior. For example, do you always remember to thank your daughter for any chores she performs at home? Do you praise her for her efforts even when she does not completely satisfy your wishes?

You are "upset" that your daughter only found fault with your husband and was not as appreciative as she should have been. In some ways, however, you may also be very critical of her shortcomings and not giving her enough credit for the gratitude she does express. The best way you can help your daughter, therefore, to improve her level of *hakaras hatov*, is to teach her by your own example how to give other people what I call "partial credit."

When I was in *yeshivah ketanah*, there were three questions we always asked our rebbi whenever a test was announced. Would it be open *Gemara* or closed *Gemara*? We always assumed the open *Gemara* tests would be easier because we could look up answers. We were wrong. Those tests were always harder.

Would the test be multiple choice or fill in? We always assumed the multiple-choice tests would be easier because we could guess if we did not know the correct answer. Again, we were wrong. Those tests were also harder.

Finally, we asked if, when grading the test papers, the rebbi would give "partial credit." In other words, if the correct answer was "Beis Hillel," and we wrote "Beis Shammai," would the rebbi take all points allotted to that question off, or would he give us some credit in recognition of our effort. After all, we did not write "Abbaye" or "Rava." From our answer it was clear we had studied for the test. Perhaps we made a careless error. At least we had some grasp of the *sugya*.

In a similar vein, we all need to learn how to give each other, and especially the members of our household, partial credit for the efforts they make on our behalf. No, it was not done exactly as we would have wanted. But if effort was made, then credit is due.

A number of years ago, I mentioned this point about partial credit at a talk I gave on *shalom bayis*. At the conclusion of the program, a woman came up to me and said, "Dr. Wikler, the point you made about partial credit went through me like a knife!" I was quite taken aback by the expression she used and asked her to explain.

She then related an incident which had taken place two weeks prior to my talk. In anticipation of sleep-over guests, she got up early on Friday morning to begin her Shabbos preparations. When she came downstairs, she was shocked to see the dining-room table fully set with china, cutlery, and stemware. Apparently, her husband had gotten up early, as well, and set the table before he left for *Shacharis*. Then she noticed that he had not used the fancier paper napkins they usually used for Shabbos.

When her husband came home, she confronted him. "Don't you know we only use these napkins for weekday?!"

He then responded, "Is that *all* you noticed about the table?" He then left for work and neither one of them made any mention of that interchange when he returned. In fact, she had completely forgotten about it until she heard my talk on partial credit. "As soon as I get home tonight," she confessed, contritely, "I plan to apologize to my husband for being so ungrateful."

It is now some years later and I am still waiting for a "thank you" from that man for straightening out his wife.

Our 17-year-old Daughter Is Severely Overweight

Our oldest daughter is 17 years old and is a senior in high school. She is a pretty and extremely talented girl. She is very bright, artistic, and creative. She has a close group of friends and does very well socially. She is also very mature in many areas of her life. For example, she knows her future career goals and has begun working toward them. She also independently (with our approval, of course) plans and implements her summer jobs, involvement in *chesed*, etc. In short, she really impresses people as a girl who is mature and "has it all put together."

However, she is 30 pounds overweight. Since she is quite short, she is considered medically obese. She gained the weight gradually because of a minor medical issue which has since been resolved. Yet, she is completely unmotivated to lose the weight. Despite our discussions, in which she acknowledges the important role of weight in *shidduchim*, she cannot resist the cake, chocolate, etc.

She does exercise, but does not combine this with portion control and therefore does not lose weight. I have offered her the opportunity to join Weight Watchers, but she refuses because she thinks she will use all her daily points on cake and junk and then starve herself.

Losing weight is hard work, but it will open many doors for her. As she is on the brink of *shidduchim*, we are at a loss as to how to motivate her. Is her lack of drive a sign of immaturity? What can we do to help her? Please advise us. Thank you.

According to the *Shulchan Aruch*, "A man is obligated to be joyous and glad on *Yom Tov* — he and his wife and children — all those who are dependent upon him. How should he make young children happy? He should give them roasted corn and nuts" (*Orach Chayim, Hilchos Yom Tov* 529:2).

From these words of the *Shulchan Aruch*, it is clear that pleasing children with edible treats is nothing new to Jewish family life. It has been going on for centuries.

Recent clinical studies, however, indicate that 20 percent of American children are significantly overweight. While there are no statistics available on the occurrence of childhood obesity among Orthodox Jews, anecdotal evidence — combined with the fact that so much of the observance of Shabbos and *Yom Tov* focuses on the family gathered around the table to partake of multicoursed *seudos* — would suggest that the incidence of childhood obesity in the *frum* community is at least as high as that among the larger American society. So, you are certainly not alone in facing this challenge.

You write that you "are at a loss as to how to motivate" your daughter. From your description, however, it appears that she is a highly motivated young lady, actively pursuing her career, employment, and *chesed* goals. While many 17-year-olds do suffer from a "lack of drive," she is certainly not one of them.

What you mean, of course, is how can you motivate your daughter to get more serious about tackling her weight problem? And this opens the door to the much broader question of how can parents motivate their children to pursue goals which the parents want for the children, but the children do not (yet) want for themselves.

Parents often yearn for their children to be more responsible, goal oriented, frustration tolerant, hard working, and well organized, when their children do not demonstrate any interest on their own to acquire these *middos*.

This often becomes an extremely frustrating endeavor for both parent and child. Parents would never dream of trying to convince a child who prefers chocolate ice cream to work on changing his preference to strawberry or vanilla. Nevertheless, these same parents will cajole, coerce, confront, and coax their children to engage in activities, projects, and programs which the parents value and the children do not.

Now before the picket line forms in front of my home, let me clarify that ice-cream flavors are *not* the same as *middos* and parents most certainly *do* have the right *and* responsibility to be *mechaneich* their children. And a major part of that *chinuch* involves guiding and teaching children how to make the right choices in life. Just as we do not allow a 2-year-old to decide for himself whether or not he should run into the street, so too, must we make other important decisions for our children.

A 17-year-old, however, is not the same as a 2-year-old. And as children mature — and your daughter sounds quite mature to me — they need to begin to make more and more decisions for themselves. This is not because they have some kind of newfangled right or modern freedom. This is because the facts on the ground are that 17-year-olds today have their own agendas in life. And trying to force our way of thinking into their agenda can sometimes cause more harm than good.

For example, you described your daughter as being "on the brink of *shidduchim*," which means that you expect her to be getting married fairly soon. She, on the other hand, may not feel ready for marriage for some reason. If so, her "lack of drive" to lose weight may really represent her unspoken wish to push off *shidduchim* for the time being. Perhaps, therefore, once she decides on her own that she is ready for *shidduchim*, she will demonstrate the motivation to lose weight that seems to be missing now.

After having said all of that, the question remains: What *can* you do to help your daughter?

The first thing you need to do is look around at home. Is anyone else in the family overweight? If either you or your spouse are overweight, you are poor role models for her. And if you cannot control your eating it will make it more difficult for your daughter to control hers.

The next thing you need to do is to recognize that the role of a parent of an adolescent is quite different — even painfully different — from the role of a parent of a younger child. With younger children, you can make most decisions for them. With adolescents, you try to facilitate and support their making the right decisions for themselves.

More specifically, regarding your daughter and her weight problem, *lectures* on obesity and *shidduchim* must be abandoned. They should be replaced by pointed, polite, and practical *questions*. For example, "Is there anything we can do to help you in dealing with your weight?"

You can also offer to pay for meetings with a nutritionist, personal trainer, or therapist, or to find a convenient meeting of Overeaters Anonymous for her to attend. You should conclude your offer of assistance with the following declaration.

"We are ready to help you with this in any way you would like. But it will be up to you to decide if and when you want us to get involved. Until that time, we will wait until you are ready."

You may feel you are abdicating your responsibility to your daughter by making that statement. By putting the control into her hands, however, you are really creating the optimum conditions for her to make the right choice for herself. And when she does so, which I believe will be sooner than you think, she will be truly self-motivated. And then her weight-loss program will be most likely to achieve a successful outcome.

We Need Guidance In Choosing a Mesivta for Our 13-Year-Old Son

Our son recently had his *bar mitzvah*. With the *simchah* behind us, my wife and I are now looking ahead to our next challenge: where to send our son for *mesivta* next year. And since the deadline for applications is fast approaching, we really must decide as soon as possible.

The *bar mitzvah* boy is the middle of our three sons. Our oldest two children are girls. One is married and the other is attending seminary in Eretz Yisrael.

The reasons choosing a *mesivta* is so complex are as follows.

My wife and I would like our son to attend the *mesivta* where his older brother is currently learning in the first year of *beis medrash*. This is a mainstream yeshivah with an excellent reputation. Our oldest son learned in the *mesivta* there and excelled in his learning. The rebbe'im and *hanhalah* are excellent. And we feel this will be a good place for our middle son to grow in his learning. Even though he is in the bottom half of his class this year, because of our connections with this yeshivah, we are confident that he would be accepted.

The problem here is that our middle son does not want to attend that *mesivta*. He would like to go to another *mesivta* that has a reputation for much lower standards in terms of learning. He says that he prefers that *mesivta* because some of his close friends are planning to go there. But we suspect his true motivation is that he imagines there will be less pressure at that *mesivta*.

My wife and I are concerned that if he goes to the *mesivta* of his choice, he will not live up to his true potential. In addition, his friends who will be going there are not exactly the better boys in his class.

Whenever we mention our reservations about his choice,

our son becomes adamant. He objects to joining his older brother, claiming that the rebbe'im will expect more of him than he is capable of producing. While he may be right about that, we see that as an advantage because the rebbe'im's expectations might motivate him to *shteig* in his learning. In addition, we like the idea of having his older brother look after him, especially during that critical first year in *mesivta*.

As we have been unable to convince our son that attending his older brother's *mesivta* would be the best thing for him, we are left with only two alternatives: (1) force him to attend the mesivta of our choice against his will; or (2) allow him to attend the lower-level *mesivta*.

I hope I have given you sufficient information to enable you to guide us. Thank you, in advance, for your advice.

A **From your letter,** it is clear that you are considering only two choices. I can assume, therefore, that there are specific reasons you have rejected all of the other options. Since you are in conflict with your son, however, that might be reason enough to reconsider the other possibilities. Perhaps there is a third *mesivta* that would satisfy all of you. In case there really are no other yeshivahs available, then I would offer you the following advice.

Shlomo HaMelech, the wisest of all men, already answered your question. As he instructed, "*chanoch l'naar al pi darko*, educate a child according to his way" (*Mishlei* 22:6). It is relevant to point out that he did not say, "according to *your* way." In other words, decisions about *chinuch* must be made with the individual needs of the child in mind and not necessarily the preferences of the parents.

Harav Shlomo Wolbe, *ztz"l*, in his classic *sefer, Z'riah U'binyan B'chinuch* (Feldheim, 1995), put it this way. "More than once we have encountered parents who place great value on things they missed in their own childhood . . . The poor child, however, has a natural tendency in another direction. Then the father crushes this inclination saying, 'You will learn what I did not.' The ultimate result is that the child loses out on both counts. What he is capable of, he is not allowed to pursue. And what he is offered, he does not want. Consequently, he is not successful" (pp. 30, 31).

It is clear that you want your son to be the best he can be. For that reason, you want him to attend the best *mesivta* that will accept him. But just because one *mesivta* has a better reputation and your older son excelled there does not mean that it is the right place for your next son.

Suppose, for the moment, that you do "force him to attend" the yeshivah where his older brother is learning. You are assuming that the influence of the excellent rebbe'im together with the prodding of his older brother will motivate your middle son to catch up and keep up with the higher standards of that yeshivah. That is what is commonly called "wishful thinking."

The much-more-likely scenario is that the higher standards and expectations of that *mesivta* may discourage your middle son. After all, he is at the bottom half of his class now, according to your letter.

More importantly, if he fails at the *mesivta* of your choice, he can always blame his failure on you. *I did not want to go there,* he may think or say, "You made me." In fact, this may even provide an added incentive for him to fail. That way he can prove that you were wrong and he was right.

If, on the other hand, you permit him to attend the *mesivta* he prefers, then the pressure is on him to succeed there. Were he not to do well at the *mesivta* of his choice, he would, in effect, be proving that he was wrong and perhaps you were right. And the distastefulness of that scenario could provide an added incentive for him to flourish at the other *mesivta*.

Many years ago, a family with whom I was working faced a similar dilemma with their daughter. Two Bais Yaakov high schools were under consideration: the one the parents preferred and the one the daughter wanted. The parents were concerned about the fact that the high school their daughter chose accepted girls from homes with lower standards. The school they liked admitted only girls from "better" homes.

The parents did not consult with me about this. And they decided on their own to insist their daughter enroll in the "better" high school, which she did. To their dismay, their daughter eventually befriended the *only* classmate from a less-than-wholesome family, who fulfilled the parents' worst nightmares by influencing their daughter in the worst imaginable direction. And it took many years, much heartache, tears and counseling until this daughter eventually returned to the fold.

In short, I do not see a real choice for you here. Forcing your son to attend the *mesivta* of your choice could prove to be a disaster. Therefore, I strongly recommend that you allow your son to attend the *mesivta* he prefers. In doing so, however, you can hedge your bets by expressing some doubt.

More specifically, you could tell him, "We're not sure if this is the best place for you. Since you want to go there, we are certainly willing to give you the opportunity to attend the *mesivta* of your choice. Then let's see how well you do there." If he succeeds at the *mesivta* of his choice, he will then enjoy the double satisfaction of personal achievement plus proving that your doubts were unjustified. And that will be a win-win situation for all of you.

Should I Offer a Job to My 17-Year-Old Nephew Who Is a Kid at Risk?

It appears as if my 17-year-old nephew has joined the ranks of "kids at risk." Needless to say, this has devastated my brother and sister-in-law together with their other four children.

Since this *machlah* struck our family, I am even more baffled as to what causes it. Some writers blame the parents. Perhaps a few abusive parents are at fault. But I know that my brother and sister-in-law, and many parents like them, bear no responsibility.

My brother is a *ben Torah/balabus* who is not a workaholic. He spends quality time with all of his children. And except for the 17-year-old, all of his other children could be poster boys and girls for their yeshivahs and Bais Yaakovs.

While I would love to hear your take on this plague in the *frum* community, I am writing to ask a more specific question. My nephew is not learning or working now. As I own a local retail store, I could offer him a job. But I am hesitant to do so because it might be embarrassing for my brother and his family if my customers see my nephew the way he is dressed. In addition, it may close the door on his ever going back to yeshivah once he enters the workforce. What would you recommend?

Chazal **teach** that "Idleness leads to insanity" (*Kesubos* 59b). It is not healthy for anyone, therefore, to have nothing meaningful and productive to do all day.

If your nephew is not in yeshivah and has no job, he is at risk of falling into depression or worse, *chalilah.* Your providing a job for him could be a life-saving act of *chesed.* With regular employment, even if only part-time, your nephew could begin the healing process of rebuilding his self-esteem. And make no mistake about it. If your nephew has dropped out of yeshivah, his self-esteem has had to have suffered a major blow.

The work, itself, would be therapeutic for your nephew. But the fact that his uncle cared enough to offer him the job, without his having to ask for it, would be an additional source of encouragement. It means you have confidence in him and you value the contribution he can make. In the short, the road to his recovery may begin with the rehabilitation that paid employment can provide.

Regarding your reasons for hesitation, they are both legitimate considerations. Just as you would not want others making decisions for your children, you should not violate your brother and sister-in-law's parental rights. You must, therefore, discuss the job offer with them, first, before approaching your nephew.

If your brother or your sister-in-law brings up the issue of your nephew's unorthodox attire, then you have two options. First, you could offer to impose a dress code on your nephew while he is working in your store. For example, if he is serving customers, you can require long pants and a collared shirt. This could be presented to him as a condition of employment.

If you suspect, however, that your nephew will resent any attempt to change his mode of dress so much that he might turn down your offer, then you must choose the second option. Try to convince your brother and sister-in-law that the benefit to your nephew of working far outweighs any negative social repercussions to them. In reality, however, neighbors probably have already seen your nephew and know what mode of attire he has adopted.

Regarding your second hesitation, your premise is somewhat faulty. Are you suggesting that by your nephew *not* working now and continuing to remain idle all day, he is *more* likely to return to Torah study than if he had a job? If so, this is simply untrue. The fact is that when at-risk-youth engage in productive, gratifying activities, they are more likely to return to Torah study and observance than their peers who continue to hang out all day.

Finally, you contend that most parents of at-risk-youth bear no responsibility for their children going off the *derech*. I must take issue with you, as well, on this point.

We all know that the first five of the *Aseres HaDibros* deal with *mitzvos* which are *bein adam l'Makom* while the last five are *bein adam l'chaveiro*. If so, the fifth *dibur* (*kibud av v'eim*) seems to be misplaced.

The lesson is that there is a direct connection between our relationships with our parents and our relationship with *HaKadosh Baruch Hu*. If we are close and devoted to them, that enables us to be close with Him. If, *chalilah*, we are at odds with them, we will feel distanced from Him as well. Faranak Margolese makes essentially this point in her groundbreaking book, *Off The Derech* (Devora Publishing, '05), which Rabbi Abraham J. Twerski M.D. called, "mandatory reading."

Harav Yaakov Perlow, the Novominsker Rebbe, *shlita*, recently said, "One thing is clear. If a child is brought up in a way that makes *Yiddishkeit geshmak* [delightful], he enjoys it, he will not tend to go off . . . Where there is *varemkeit* [warmth] in the home then he enjoys the Shabbos, enjoys speaking to his parents" (*Hamodia Magazine,* Nov. 24, '10, p. 29).

A dramatic demonstration of the impact of family dynamics on the level of religious observance of at-risk-youth took place in my office not too long ago. In order to appreciate that episode, however, a little background information is necessary.

A colleague of mine began treating an 18-year-old yeshivah dropout. The young man had stopped learning and davening and even refused to participate in the *seudos* of Shabbos. To reinforce the individual therapy he was providing, my colleague referred the parents to me for guidance regarding their day-to-day interactions with their son.

As any *frum* parents, they were distraught over their son's lack of observance — and even disparagement — of *mitzvos*. While they were not especially critical people, they still needed to exercise great restraint not to find fault with his more flagrant, provocative violations of a Torah lifestyle. To their credit, however, for the next two years, they followed my directions, eliminating critical words from their vocabulary and replacing them with sincere praise.

One day, the young man asked his parents if they wanted him to join them in my office. This did not come completely out of the blue. His parents had not kept their meetings with me a secret from their other children. And on more than one occasion, they had invited him to join them. The parental guidance suddenly morphed into regular family therapy.

In one of the family-therapy sessions, the mother began telling her son how proud she was of his recent completion of college courses. She also praised his success in landing a part-time job. Then, in the most casual manner imaginable, he pulled a yarmulke from his pocket and placed it on his formerly bare head. None of the four of us commented on that striking display of reconciliation. The last one to leave my office after that session was the father who flashed a silent grin to me while making the gesture of thumbs up! And for every session thereafter, the son continued to wear his yarmulke.

That critical incident in the family-therapy session illustrates an important dynamic of the kids-at-risk phenomenon. When rebellious or acting out young people are made to feel loved and accepted, especially by their parents, they tend to reduce the intensity of their rejection of their parents' values. And, in some cases, they may even return to those very same values.

Returning to your letter, therefore, you must see your offer of a job to your nephew as a loud declaration of your love and acceptance of him. And as long as his parents are O.K. with it, your offering him a job at your store could be the first important step in his rehabilitation. Once your nephew feels that his uncle cares enough about him to give him a job, and once he tastes the satisfaction of being productive, he may find the motivation to begin to turn his life around.

Your nephew is most fortunate to have an uncle who is as concerned and loving as you are. If more kids at risk had uncles (or brothers, cousins or grandparents) like you, then I believe that we would have far fewer kids at risk.

Our 13-Year-Old Son
Ran Away to My Parents' Home

We have enjoyed reading your column each week and gain valuable insights on parenting. But we never thought we would have to write to you, ourselves. Unfortunately, a recent crisis with our 13-year-old son has prompted us to turn to you for advice.

He is the fifth of our six children and has always been a difficult child. Because of his unusual restlessness in preschool, his teacher recommended a psychological evaluation. The psychologist found that he had above-average intelligence and good concentration. However, he was also found to be impatient, "overconfident, and tested the limits."

More recently, he is unhappy and does not have close friends. He is not motivated to learn and performs well below his abilities. His attendance at yeshivah is poor, coming late often and occasionally not going at all. We had thought that once he would get past the pressures of his *bar mitzvah*, he would settle down somewhat. Unfortunately, that did not happen.

At home, he is *chutzpadik* and disobedient. We would love for him to meet with a therapist. But he adamantly rejects the idea whenever we mention it.

Last week, I told him that he needed to get a haircut. He refused. In trying to set firm limits, I told him that in order to live in our home, he would have to conform to some basic rules, one of which was to get a haircut. He then impulsively ran over to my parents' home and has been staying there ever since.

My parents do not want to undermine our authority in any way. They called me immediately and offered to insist that he return home. They have also tried, unsuccessfully, to convince him to speak with a therapist. And they even promised him a monetary bribe. But he still refused.

So far, I have told them to let him stay. I am afraid if they kick him out, he may not come home. And then I would not know where he might end up. In addition, they have told me that he is attending yeshivah regularly and on time since he has been living with them.

My husband and I did go over to my parents' home the next day to try to speak with our son. But he locked himself in his room, refusing to come out. He was unwilling to talk with us and only shouted from behind the closed door that we should go away.

My questions for you are: Do you think my parents should continue to allow him to stay in their home and, if so, for how long? Also, would you recommend that my parents try to set limits for him in their home? We very much want our son back home with us but we also want to do what is best for him.

Thank you, in advance, for your advice.

Before I answer your serious and pressing questions, I must acknowledge how painful this entire episode must be for you and your husband. You are obviously caring and conscientious parents. Having taken your son for a psychological evaluation so many years ago clearly testifies to your above-average dedication to the welfare of your children. And the fact that your son has, in effect, run away from home must feel more hurtful than a slap in the face. I commend you on your ability to reach out for guidance during this crisis rather than lash out in desperation.

Your son, of course, must also be in great pain. After all, to have taken such a drastic step, he must have been feeling quite desperate.

Now to your questions. If your parents are willing to allow your son to stay with them, then by all means they should continue to do so. Your son, after all, did choose their home. And apparently, from what you wrote, it appears that living with them is having a positive influence on him.

While it is certainly understandable why you and your parents would want to set limits on your son's behavior, one must always consider the unintended consequences of any action. By your parents imposing conditions or standards of conduct on your son, you are hoping that they will succeed in straightening him out. That is certainly a most worthwhile goal. There is no reason to suspect, however, that your parents' experience with that approach will be any different from yours.

When you attempted to set limits on your son by giving him the ultimatum of getting a haircut or leaving your home, he chose the latter. Please do not misunderstand me. I am not an advocate of long hairstyles for yeshivah boys. But a child who rejects parental authority does not usually welcome limit-setting with outstretched arms, even from his grandparents.

Just because your parents are not setting rules for your son, however, does not mean they are not having a positive influence on him. The fact that he has voluntarily chosen to attend yeshivah regularly while in their home attests to his desire to please them. While this positive influence is not as concrete and demonstrable as setting limits, it may, in the long run, be even more effective.

But doesn't a 13-year-old boy belong at home with his parents?!

Sure. Sometimes, however, a temporary "time-out" is really the healthiest approach to dealing with a potentially explosive family conflict. If your parents' home is a wholesome one — and I have no reason to suspect that it is not — then this current arrangement may be the best solution under the current circumstances. Since the *Gemara* teaches us that "Grandchildren are like children" (*Yevamos* 62b), then grandparents make the best surrogate parents.

Parashas Mishpatim begins with the laws pertaining to an *eved ivri* (*Shemos* 21:2). On that *pasuk*, Rashi tells us that the Torah is referring to a thief who has been sold by a *beis din* to repay that which he has stolen.

What is the rationale for selling a Jewish thief into slavery?

Rabbi Shamshon Rephael Hirsch, in his commentary on the Torah, explains as follows. "The Torah . . . orders the criminal to be brought into the life of a family as we might order a refractory child to be brought under the influence of Jewish family life . . . He should still feel himself considered and treated as a brother, capable of being loved and giving love."

In the healing environment of his grandparents' loving home, therefore, your son may experience exactly the rehabilitation he so desperately needs. And just as the Jewish slave must remain in the home of his master for six years to complete his reformation, so too, your son may need to stay with his grandparents for — hopefully less than six years, but — longer than you would want. I recommend, therefore, that you allow your son to remain with his grandparents until he feels ready to return to your home.

In the meantime, you might want to send your son a brief letter indicating that you are ready and willing to take him back, without preconditions, whenever he feels ready to return home.

While you are primarily focused now (and rightly so) on your 13-year-old, you gave no indication in your letter as to how your other five children are reacting to this major development at home. Do they know where he is, why he left, and what you are doing about it? If so, did they learn this from you, your parents, or from him? In addition, have you discussed this with them at all?

Generally speaking, it is comforting for children of all ages to know that their parents are not helpless, ineffective, and avoiding problems. And it is reassuring for them to see that their parents are, at least, aware of and trying to deal with problems, even if they are not capable of immediately solving them.

I would recommend, therefore, that even if your other children have not broached the subject of the whereabouts of your 13-year-old, you should raise it with them. Do not go into great detail, but do tell them where he is, that he chose to go there, and you are in close communication with your parents about it. This will then open the door for them to share any concerns they have with you rather than to suppress them which could create unnecessary stress for them.

Our Son, Who Is Away in Yeshivah, Is Not Very Social, Is Stubborn, and Very Argumentative

Perhaps you could help me. I feel very frustrated.

Our son, the youngest in the family, has a problem. And he is not the first in our family to have this problem. In yeshivah he prefers learning by himself without any *chavrusos*. Nevertheless, he is very bright and thorough in his learning. He will not just *lein* through his learning without understanding it.

In addition, he is not very social. Since he was younger, he never told me the names of his friends. None of his friends visit him nor does he visit them. And when I ask him who his friends are, he does not want to tell me.

Furthermore, he has very strong likes and dislikes regarding food. And he is very particular, in general. He has his own mind about things and is very stubborn about his opinions. He can sit and argue with someone about issues to the point of exhaustion. In fact, the way he argues his point makes me think he could be a lawyer.

Although I love him very much because he is my son, I feel I have nothing in common with him. There is nothing I share with him about which I can have a conversation. Whenever he calls home from yeshivah, which he does quite often, I have to rack my brain to come up with neutral topics to discuss. And I have to be careful to avoid topics that could cause an argument.

Regarding the *chavrusa* issue, I have referred my son to Rav Wolbe's *Aleh Shor*. But he is impervious to my arguments.

I am a concerned mother and am eagerly anticipating your advice.

Before I respond to your inquiry, I must address what was omitted from your letter. You have made no reference to your husband's opinion of and experience with your son. His assessment of and interaction with your son may be very similar to yours. Nevertheless, even subtle differences could be helpful in unraveling the mystery of your son's behavior.

As *Chazal* have taught, "There are three partners in [the creation of] man: *HaKadosh Baruch Hu*, his father, and his mother" (*Kiddushin* 30b). To leave out your husband's perspective, therefore, is to disregard one third of the equation.

Very often, for example, a child may manifest the same problematic behavior with both parents. With one parent, however, the problem is slightly more pronounced while with the other parent the issue is somewhat diminished. In such cases, that information is extremely helpful and contributes greatly to making an accurate diagnosis.

From what you have written, however, it is clear that your son has a significant social problem and is not *m'urav im habri'os*. The fact that he learns well on his own should not mask the troublesome deficit he seems to have in social skills.

In all probability, the different areas of your concern are all interconnected. If your son is as stubbornly opinionated as you portray him to be, then it stands to reason that he would fail to make and keep good friends. No one enjoys the company of someone who is uncompromising, self-centered, and rigid. Such people are perceived as rejecting and treated likewise. As Shlomo HaMelech declared, "Just as water reflects, so too does a man respond to his fellow in the manner in which he is treated" (*Mishlei* 27:19).

If he has failed to make and keep good friends, your son might feel the need to conceal that from you for fear of criticism and/or embarrassment.

Finally, if he cannot maintain friendships, then your son would have an even tougher time landing *chavrusos*. Left with no alternative, he might convince himself that he "prefers" to learn alone. Or, he could be so self-absorbed that he would truly rather learn without another person around to challenge, confront or even question his understanding of the *Gemara*.

It appears that your son is already living in a dormitory at *mesivta* or *beis medrash*. If so, then he is too old for you to insist he enter therapy. Furthermore, since he is so sure of himself, he would be very unlikely to agree to meet with anyone who might try to help him.

Since you will be unable to modify *his* behavior, your only option at this point is to modify *yours* in dealing with him. Hopefully, however, if you implement the following recommendations carefully, you may succeed in penetrating your son's thick wall of denial and resistance.

Just as it takes two to fight, it requires two sides to argue. Therefore, you must deliberately avoid bringing up discussion topics that could cause an argument. The subsequent quarrels would be counterproductive. If you do enter into debates with him, you would be reinforcing and rewarding the very behavior you want to extinguish. Instead of challenging his opinions, you should simply not respond to them.

Do not worry that your silence could be misconstrued as agreement. Your son already knows you disagree with him on many issues. If you make any attempt to dissuade him, you will only provoke him to become more argumentative and reinforce his stubbornness.

Are you then simply supposed to listen passively? Absolutely not. You should take advantage of the opportunity to become an active listener.

Active listening is a two-step process that demonstrates that you are paying attention and trying to understand what your son — or any other family member, for that matter — is saying.

The first step is reflecting, which means that you repeat back to your son, in your own words, whatever you hear him say. We find an excellent example of this in *Tanach*, where Shlomo HaMelech repeats the claims of the two mothers vying for custody of the same baby. (See *Melachim* I 3:23 and the commentaries on that *pasuk*, especially the Malbim.)

The second step is asking good questions. Be sure that the questions are designed to elicit more information from your son, such as, "What makes you feel that way?" or "Why is that important to you?" When asking questions, however, it is crucial that your tone of voice not convey a challenge or an objection, such as, "Do you *really* think that is *so* important?" or "How *could* you *possibly* think that way?"

You are not required to agree with anything your son tells you. Whenever you disagree, however, that should be kept to yourself, enabling you to focus in on really hearing what your son has to say.

Even if your son does not abandon any of his stubbornly held opinions, your active listening will cease your frustrating, endless arguments and will eliminate your problem of finding "neutral topics to discuss."

The larger issue here, however, is that your son seems to lack sufficient social skills to enable him to interact comfortably with others. Your relationship with him is certainly important. Now that he is away at yeshivah, however, and living in the dormitory, a way must be found to smooth out some of his rough edges.

I would recommend, therefore, that you and/or your husband speak with his rebbe'im and/or *mashgiach*. Have they observed the same problems you described in your letter? If so, are they worried? Are they trying to help him in any way? What would they recommend? Sometimes a phone call like that from a concerned parent helps the yeshivah address a problem which warrants their attention but may have not yet fully appeared on their radar screens.

For example, they are in an excellent position to encourage your son to become more social. They could recommend that he learn for at least one *seder* with a *chavrusa*. They could grant him privileges or assign responsibilities that would require him to interact more with his peers. Or, they could arrange for him to meet with one of their rebbe'im or a private therapist who would help him to improve his social skills. Even if they do not come up with a creative solution, however, hearing their observations and perspective may enable you to come up with your own.

My 17-Year-Old Always Wants My Company

I have a 17-year-old son. When he is home after school, he always wants my company. And he wants me to be in the same room with him. If I go into another room to take care of whatever I need, he'll say, "Why are you running away from me?" Or, if he does go into another room to go on the computer, for example, he'll suddenly ask if I can go there so he can show me something. And he'll call out, "Mommy, come!"

Usually, boys at this age want to do their own thing and like their independence. He does have a good friend in school. But once he comes home, he does not invite any neighborhood friends to come over to our house. Still, I would think that he could occupy himself without needing my presence all the time.

What do I do about his constant calling me? It drives me crazy. And, yes, he gets counseling. But these behaviors continue. I'd like to hear your opinion. Please answer ASAP.

As *Chazal* have taught, "Hearing is not comparable to seeing" (*Mechilta, Parashas Yisro*, 19:9). Or, as the saying goes, "Seeing is believing." The opinion and recommendations of your son's therapist, therefore, are far more valuable than mine because he has seen your son and I have not. And since you did not include in your letter any comments or instructions from your son's therapist, I must assume that you have had little or no communication with him. So let me begin with a crash course in how to remedy that situation.

Even though your son is a minor and you have a legal right to have access to all of his medical and mental-health records, it is in the best interests of your son's therapy that his privacy be respected as much as possible. In order for your son to succeed in his work with the therapist, he must establish a strong therapeutic bond based on mutual trust. You absolutely cannot, therefore, attempt to communicate with your son's therapist behind your son's back. Even if the therapist would agree to do so, you should not consent to that arrangement because it would eventually undermine the therapy.

The first step, therefore, is for you to approach your son and tell him that you would like to speak with his therapist. If he asks why, tell him that you would like guidance from the therapist on how you can be a better parent to him. If he does not ask why, tell him anyway. If he does not ask and you do not explain the reason for your wanting to speak with his therapist, he may suspect that your agenda is to bad-mouth him in some way.

If your son refuses to grant you permission, explore the reasons for his objection. Ask him what his concerns are. What is he afraid would happen if you did communicate with the therapist? If your son stubbornly refuses even to share his rationale for not wanting you to speak with his therapist, at least get him to agree to discuss the matter at his next session. That way the therapist can explore issues that your son may not feel comfortable discussing with you.

If your son does agree to your speaking with his therapist, then give your son the choice of whether or not he would like to be present. This is an extremely important part of the process. If your son is apprehensive about your meeting his therapist, his fears will be allayed greatly by being in attendance at the meeting. And even if he chooses not to attend, which is the more likely scenario, he will be reassured because you gave him the option to do so.

Once you have obtained your son's permission, call his therapist and explain the process up to that point. Then schedule an appointment to meet with the therapist. A meeting is always preferable to a phone call because, for important matters such as this, face-to-face communication facilitates the mutual understanding needed for a successful consultation.

When you do finally sit down with your son's therapist, try not to focus too much on your own frustration. Instead, use the time more productively by asking your questions. And make sure that you steer clear of prying into your son's privacy.

For example, do not ask, "What does he talk to you about?" or, "What does he tell you about me?" Instead, ask, "Is there anything you have discussed with my son that you feel I should know about?" or, "Is there anything about my son that you feel I am misunderstanding or mishandling at home?"

Then proceed to ask the questions that prompted you to call. For example, "How would you recommend that I handle it whenever my son follows me around the house?" or, "What do you feel I should say whenever my son complains that I am running away from him if I simply go into another room to take care of something?"

A word of warning is in order here. Some adolescent therapists may not agree to meet with you even if you have your son's permission. They may also refuse to counsel you over the phone. If your son's therapist takes that approach, do not become alarmed. It is not an indication of incompetence, inexperience or insecurity. Rather, it is based on the perfectly legitimate concern that your son may have felt coerced into agreeing to let you speak with the therapist because you are paying! Your son may not feel comfortable about it but may feel he has no choice other than to agree.

The therapist, therefore, may feel he must advocate for your son's unspoken preference. It is also possible that your son told you it was O.K., while confiding to the therapist his true feelings on the matter. Finally, the therapist may also not want to offer you any parenting advice because he is concerned that doing so would compromise the therapeutic relationship of trust he has worked so hard to establish with your son.

Suppose, for example, the therapist advises you to set limits with your son. Your son could interpret that as indicating a lack of empathy and caring on the part of the therapist. And it could make your son feel that the therapist is more aligned with you than with him, even though the recommendation was made with his best interests in mind.

If your son's therapist adheres to that school of thought, from where should you get the answers to your very pressing and valid questions? How can you bring some sanity back into your home? You could call a parenting hotline, such as the Yitty Leibel Hotline at (718) HELP-NOW, consult with another therapist, or write to Partners in Parenting, which you have done.

Next week, *b'ezras Hashem*, I will offer you my own recommendations for what you can do at home to help modify your son's behavior.

My 17-Year-Old
Always Wants My Company — Part II

Last week, the mother of a 17-year-old boy wrote in, describing her son's behavior of constantly clinging to her whenever he is at home. Even though he is getting counseling, there has been no improvement, thus far, and the mother asked for my opinion.

The first installment of my answer included detailed instructions regarding how she should be communicating with her son's therapist. Today, I shall offer my assessment of her son's behavior, which she described as, "driving [her] crazy."

As stated last week, any advice or recommendations you receive from your son's therapist should be given precedence over what I am about to suggest. And I am only offering my opinion in the event that you are unable to consult with your son's therapist, either because your son will not grant you permission to do so or because the therapist will not allow it.

We recently celebrated the joyous *Yom Tov* of Succos. The *mishnah* (*Succah* 2:8) states, "A boy who does not need his mother is obligated in [the *mitzvah* of sitting in the] *succah*."

What does "not needing his mother" mean? Don't all children need their mother, regardless of their age? The classical commentator, Rav Ovadiah MiBartenura, offers the following clarification. "Every [boy] who gets up from sleeping and does not call, 'Mommy!' is [considered as one who] does not need his mother and is obligated [to fulfill the *mitzvah* of sitting in the *succah*, *mi'd'rabbanan*, for purposes of *chinuch*]. [One who is] younger than that is exempt. And so is the *halachah*. [This refers] specifically to [a situation in which] he calls out repeatedly and does not quiet down until his mother comes to him. That is one who is called needing his mother. But one who calls out once and then is quiet is not one who [is considered] needing his mother."

The *Meleches Shlomo* brings the view of *Chazal* that this corresponds to the approximate age of 6 or 7. According to *Chazal*, therefore, a child of 6 or 7 should be mature enough to sleep in the *succah* without his mother and not suffer any undo anxiety at being separated from her.

Using the *mishnah* in *Succah*, then, as a frame of reference, it is clear that your son's inability to occupy himself in another room without your company is a manifestation of significant immaturity and inappropriate dependency.

Your task, therefore, is to speak to and treat your son in ways that will promote age-appropriate independence and discourage his excessive dependence.

Whenever you speak with your son, for example, you should attempt to elicit his opinion. Ask him what he thinks about anything and everything. Then validate his opinions if they make sense and do not comment at all if they don't.

On the other hand, whenever he asks you for your opinion, resist sharing your ideas, advice, and suggestions. Instead of simply refusing to answer, which could make him feel rejected, tell him you are not sure. You need to think about it. Or, what he is asking is difficult and not so simple. Then throw the question back at him. If he says, "But if I knew what to do, I wouldn't be asking you!" you can reply, "Well, that is a difficult question for me, too."

If your son is forced to solve his own problems, make his own choices, and decide his own priorities, that will go a long way toward encouraging his independence.

A second strategy for promoting independence is to give your son more responsibility, especially at home. He should be given chores that he can complete according to his own schedule and in his own way. For example, ask him to do some of the weekly shopping. Let him choose which stores to patronize and when it is most convenient for him to make the purchases. Ask him to run errands for you. If the errands require using the family car, that will add an extra incentive for him to comply.

Doing chores and meeting responsibilities builds self-esteem and self-confidence which, in turn, can promote independence. What you are trying to do is nudge your son along the developmental path away from the dependence of childhood toward the relative independence of adolescence.

Now, I will address the specific immature behavior you described in your letter and what you can do to modify it.

Chazal have taught, "If you attempt to seize too much, you will not achieve anything. If you try to grasp a little, you will succeed" (*Rosh Hashanah* 4b). And there is nowhere where that applies more than with regard to parenting.

If you are dealing with an objectionable behavior displayed by one of your children and you attempt to eliminate it completely, overnight, you will most likely fail to achieve your goal. If, however, you minimize your expectations and aim for more modest improvement, you are much more likely to make progress.

Let's apply that principle to your situation. Whenever your son is at home, he wants you to be in the same room with him. And whenever you leave the room to take care of something, he says, "Why are you running away from me?"

The next time he is at home, instead of trying to "sneak" into the next room and "hope" he does not notice, warn him in advance and include a gentle challenge as follows. "I have to go into the next room now, but I'll come back to join you shortly. Let's see how long you can stay here, by yourself, before you come in to join me or call me back to join you." Then leave, make note of the time, and see how long it takes until he comes in after you or asks you to return to him. This may sound like a technique that is more appropriate for a 7-year-old, not a 17-year-old. If your son is acting like seven, however, it may be exactly what he needs.

Then the next time you have to leave the room, for any reason, present the challenge to your son like this. "Yesterday, when I left the room we were in together, you were able to be by yourself for 11 minutes before you called me to come back. I have to go into the kitchen now for a few minutes. Let's see if you can remain here without my company for more than 11 minutes today."

The thought of remaining in a room without you indefinitely may be too difficult for your son right now. So he follows you around or calls you back right away. If, however, he attempted merely to *stretch* the length of time he occupies himself alone, he may be able, eventually, to build up to a more appropriate level of tolerance of the separation from you while he is at home.

My Vindictive Ex-Wife Is Alienating Our Two Teenage Children From Me

Eleven years ago, I went through a messy divorce. My ex-wife has custody of our two children and I have visitation rights.

Since our divorce, I have been dragged into court on numerous occasions by my vindictive ex-wife who has claimed that I am not giving her adequate child support. Each time the judge has ruled in my favor but the legal fees I am forced to pay to defend myself have been financially draining.

Initially, we worked out all of the child support and visitation agreements with a *beis din*. But after I gave her the *get*, my ex-wife decided to go to secular court to see if she could get a better deal, which she did.

Over the years, my ex-wife has repeatedly bad-mouthed me to our children and has put stumbling blocks in the path of my visitation. She has done everything she could do to make it difficult for me to see my children, such as canceling at the last minute or calling me at the last minute to tell me that I can come right now or not at all.

In spite of all of this, I have kept up with both of my children. And I have tried to stay involved as much as possible in their lives.

My son, who is 19, is currently learning out of town and only comes home for *Yom Tov* and *Shabbos Mevarchim*. My daughter is 16 and attends a local *Bais Yaakov* high school.

Last year, before he left for yeshivah, I took my son to a restaurant. I asked him point-blank why he was not returning my phone calls. He said, "When I avoid you, Mommy loves me. And I know you will always love me unconditionally."

What prompted me to write to you now was something that took place last week in court. My wife had filed a motion to block my visitation on the grounds that I am an unfit father. And the judge had asked to speak with my children in his chambers in the presence of my ex-wife and myself. That meeting took place last week. Responding to the judge's queries, both of my children supported my ex-wife's claims.

I am now feeling extremely hurt, resentful, and betrayed by both of my children. After all I have been through for them, I would have expected at least some evenhandedness on their part, if not outright backing. I am wondering now, however, whether I am being too harsh in my judgment of my children and I would like your objective opinion on this matter.

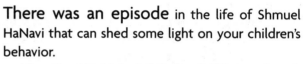

There was an episode in the life of Shmuel HaNavi that can shed some light on your children's behavior.

After Shaul HaMelech failed to fulfill the *mitzvah* of destroying Amalek (*Devarim* 25:19), Hashem told Shmuel HaNavi to anoint one of the sons of Yishai as king to replace Shaul. Upon receiving this *nevuah*, Shmuel replied, "How can I go? When Shaul hears [about this], he will kill me" (*I Shmuel* 16:2).

Taken in context, this *pasuk* seems to imply that Shmuel was afraid of Shaul's reaction. Could Shmuel truly be concerned about any human being's response to his carrying out the Will of Hashem?!

According to the Gemara (*Pesachim* 8b), that is precisely what was troubling Shmuel. But, asks the Gemara, "Does Rabbi Elazar not say that 'messengers performing *mitzvos* are never injured?'" [And, certainly, if Shmuel was carrying out the Will of Hashem, he could be considered a messenger performing a *mitzvah*.]

The Gemara then answers, "Wherever danger is to be expected is different [and that principle does not apply]; as it is said, 'And Shmuel said, How can I go? When Shaul hears [about it], he will kill me. And Hashem said [to Shmuel], Take a calf from the herd [as an offering] in your hand . . .'"

Hashem does not rebuke Shmuel, giving him a *mussar shmuess* on having more *bitachon*, trusting that all will go well. He does not criticize Shmuel for worrying unnecessarily. Rather, Hashem gives Shmuel a strategy for protecting himself from possible harm. By doing so, Hashem was validating Shmuel's concern and teaching us the principle articulated by the Gemara that the special protection due to those who are sent on *mitzvah* missions does not extend to inherently dangerous situations.

Your children also see themselves in an inherently dangerous situation. You described your ex-wife as "vindictive." In addition, you characterized your divorce as "messy." Finally, you quoted your son as acknowledging the risk he faces if he would openly support you, in any way. To protect themselves from their malevolent mother, therefore, it is most understandable that both of your children would decline to stick up for you in the judge's chambers.

Your expectations were, to put it bluntly, totally unrealistic. Your children live with their mother and not with you. Even your son spends his off-Shabbosim at his mother's home. Both of your children, therefore, have much too much at stake to publicly support you over their mother, regardless of how much you may feel entitled to the vindication.

The best thing you can do for them at this time is not to pressure them to do that which cannot be expected of them. As long as they are living with their mother, they cannot say or do anything that might threaten their relationship with her. Just as Shmuel was justified in fearing Shaul's wrath, so too, your children have good reason to be concerned about their mother's possible retribution for what she would undoubtedly regard as their disloyalty to her.

This does not mean that your children must deny your love forever. *B'ezras Hashem*, five years from now, they will be married with homes of their own. Then they will be free to act more independently, establishing the relationships with you that they choose and not what will please their mother.

I recall one couple with whom I worked almost 30 years ago. After their divorce, the man was incredibly spiteful toward his ex-wife, turning their three pre-*bar-mitzvah* age sons, of whom he had custody, against her. He withheld visitation of the boys even though the two girls, who were living with their mother, visited him regularly.

After a few months, he relented and sent his sons to his ex-wife for visitation. They had been so corrupted by their father that they literally terrorized their mother and sisters during the visit. And they even vandalized their mother's apartment during their "playful" spree of disruption.

Before responding, this woman consulted with me. She vented to me her frustration with her ex-husband, adding that she would like to let her sons know how truly rotten their father is. I empathized with her and validated her feelings. Then I explained to her that we can never hope to change other people. We can only control our reactions to them. I also told her that if she ever hoped to have a normal, healthy relationship with her sons, she should resist the impulse to bad-mouth her ex-husband to them. Right or wrong, he is their father and it will only prove detrimental if they have negative feelings about him. To her credit, she followed my advice.

Eight years later, she called to thank me. Her oldest son had called in tears from his yeshivah dormitory, begging her to forgive him for his earlier misbehavior.

Since then, her younger sons have reinitiated contact in the same way. All her boys are married now, have little or nothing to do with their father, and all enjoy a close, warm relationship with their mother, sisters, and their mother's new husband. And after the youngest son married, recently, she called to thank me, once again, for the advice I had given her so many years ago.

My Cousin, Who Was Mistreated by His Fourth-Grade Rebbi, Has Now Become a Kid at Risk

I have learned a lot from your weekly column and I am very grateful. However, the tone of your May __th article disturbed me.

You told a horrific story of how you were treated in yeshivah by your *menahel* and eighth-grade rebbi. You made light of the whole episode. It almost sounded as if you were downplaying the impact that poor judgment of *mechanchim* can have on their *talmidim*.

I have a first cousin who was severely mistreated by his fourth-grade rebbi. As a result, he has become another sad statistic of kids at risk. In fact, I'm not even sure if my cousin is still *shomer Shabbos*.

I am not suggesting that every kid at risk had rebbe'im like my cousin had or that *mechanchim* are all to blame for the growing problem of kids at risk today. But I do believe poor *chinuch* does play a role in some kids going off the *derech*. And minimizing the issue, as you did, only contributes to the problem.

Complex problems rarely have single causes or simple solutions. And the problem of kids at risk today is certainly a complex problem.

Undiagnosed learning disabilities, early childhood traumas, stressful family dynamics, and internet abuses are only some of the root causes of this terrible scourge. In addition, as you have pointed out, mistreatment by *mechanchim* can also play a role.

By and large, most *mosdos hachinuch* do an outstanding job of educating our children. And the *mechanchim* who work tirelessly to teach Torah to the next generation deserve our praise, support, and gratitude, in addition to higher salaries.

Not all people, however, are qualified for every occupation. As *Chazal* have taught, "*Lo hakapdan m'lameid*, one with an exacting personality should not serve as a rebbi" (*Pirkei Avos* 2:4).

If one is somewhat strict, why should that preclude his becoming a *mechaneich*? As the *Tiferes Yisrael* comments, "One who is stern and short tempered is not fit to teach students because . . . how can the student pay attention [and absorb] the words of someone he hates."

I do agree with you, therefore, that the harsh approaches utilized by a very few *mechanchim* have contributed to some young people becoming kids at risk. If I gave the impression that I believe otherwise, I welcome the opportunity now to set the record straight.

I also agree with you that unqualified *mechanchim* account for a very small percentage of the kids-at-risk population. There are, for example, many children who were mistreated by teachers and never went off the *derech*. That does not mean that I condone mistreatment of children. Rather, it should place this factor in proper perspective, as the following anecdote will illustrate.

Several years ago, I met a middle-aged, *frum* man who lives in one of the main Orthodox enclaves in the New York Metropolitan area. "Do you ever lecture to *mechanchim*?" he asked.

"Whenever I am invited," I replied, wondering where this conversation was headed.

"Then I would like to share with you my personal story," he began, somewhat haltingly.

"I grew up out of town, in a solidly *frum*, American home. I attended an English-speaking day school until I was 12. My parents wanted me to have a better Torah education than I could receive at the day school, so they sent me to a yeshivah in New York.

"Even though I was old enough to enter the eighth grade, I was placed in the fifth grade because I had such a weak background. In the middle of the year, I was 'promoted' to the seventh grade because I was catching up so quickly.

"The seventh-grade rebbi, unlike the one I had in fifth grade, spoke only

Yiddish. I did not understand a single word. Looking back now, I realize, I should have complained about this to my parents. But at the time, I felt I would simply make an effort to catch on as quickly as I could.

"After one or two weeks in the seventh grade, I was getting by in *Gemara* with whatever I could figure out from the Hebrew, which is interspersed with the Aramaic, from the context and from asking other boys. Then, one morning, the rebbi announced *chazarah*, which he did every day for a few minutes, during which individual students could approach his desk to ask any questions they had.

"I was hesitant to take advantage of this opportunity because I was somewhat shy at the time. But I fortified myself with the words of *Chazal*, "*Ein habayshan lomeid*, a bashful person cannot [succeed] in learning" (*Pirkei Avos* 4:2). So I waited until the rebbi was free and then walked up to his desk.

"I had the gist of the *Gemara* we had just learned. But since the rebbi translated only in Yiddish, I did not understand the last line at all. So I asked him to review the last line of the *Gemara*.

"The rebbi then *klopped* on his desk to get the entire class's attention and announced in a loud, booming voice in Yiddish, 'I want everyone to hear what the *shoteh* (fool) and *tipeish she'ein kamohu* (incredible idiot) just asked!'"

"At the time, I did not understand what he said. But I knew enough to realize that the words *shoteh* and *tipeish* were derogatory expressions. When I found out later what those words meant, I was retroactively mortified.

"To say that the rest of that year was completely destroyed for me would be an understatement. In fact, I don't think I really got back to myself until I was about 16. I was a shy kid to begin with and what the rebbi did to me that day really broke me.

"In those days, I guess it wasn't 'in' to go off the *derech*. So I remained *frum*, as you can see, up to this day. After that episode, however, I was never able to really learn. And that is still a problem for me.

"You might be wondering: Why am I telling you my whole life story now? Since I know you are a public speaker and you just told me that you sometimes speak to *mechanchim*, I thought you might be able to use my story as an example of how much damage a *mechaneich* can do if he is not suited for *chinuch*."

While I do speak publicly to *mechanchim* and lay audiences, I have hesitated telling that man's story because it is such an extreme case. I have decided to share it now, however, for two reasons.

First, this personal, painful account illustrates how someone can suffer the most outrageous mistreatment in yeshivah and still not go off the *derech*. All of his children, for example, are attending and doing well at mainstream *mosdos hachinuch*.

The mistreatment this man received from his seventh-grade rebbi was inexcusable. And it clearly would have shaken up any 12-year-old boy. Whether one goes off the *derech*, however, depends on other factors, as well. One boy may have supportive, loving friendships which soften the blow of such emotional traumas, while another boy may have none. One boy may have innate confidence, while another boy tends to be more sensitive. In each case, therefore, it is the sum total of strengths and supports versus weaknesses and assaults which determine which children will go off the *derech* and which will not.

When a bridge collapses, for example, people rush to point the finger of blame at someone. Were the bridge inspectors negligent in their duties? Were their supervisors bribed or lax in their oversight? Or, was the original design flawed to begin with? More often than not, a *combination* of factors resulted in the failure of the bridge to support its weight. By taking all contributing factors into consideration, therefore, we can avoid the pitfall of overly simplifying a multifaceted and complex problem.

Secondly, my publicizing this narrative should eliminate any doubt in your mind, or in the mind of any reader, that I fully appreciate the fact that serious, long-term damage can be promulgated by misguided, unqualified *mechanchim*.

Our 13-Year-Old Son
Can Be Extremely Stubborn

My wife and I have a question regarding our 13-year-old son. He is the second of our six children and really is a very good boy. He gets along well with his classmates as well as his siblings. He earns good grades in both English and Hebrew subjects. And he is generally a gentle, mild-mannered child.

What bothers us, however, is that he can be, at times, extremely stubborn. Even in situations where his stubbornness will end up hurting him, he still will not back down.

This past Shabbos, for example, my wife gave out ices for dessert. As we had guests at the table and there were only eight ices in the package, my wife announced that everyone would only get half of a portion. Our 13-year-old insisted that he wanted a whole one. My wife calmly explained that there were not enough in the package for everyone to get a whole ice. He remained inflexible and unyielding in his demand. Finally, my wife informed him that he had only two choices: Either accept a half or take none at all. He chose the latter, but was visibly unhappy about it.

Our question, therefore, is twofold. First, we are wondering whether or not we handled the episode correctly. For example, since he was so upset, should my wife have given in and let him have a whole one? And, secondly, what advice can you give us for dealing with such a child?

As has been pointed out many times in this column, all children are born with distinct personalities and unique character traits with which they were genetically endowed. These traits are not the result of parenting or environmental factors. Just as two children from the same family can have different-colored eyes and hair, two children from the same family can have different natures. One child may be flexible and easy going while another is obstinate and bull headed.

The most important thing you must bear in mind is that parents cannot change a child's innate character traits. Harav Yisroel Salanter, *ztz"l*, once said that the hardest thing in the world to change is a *middah*. And he said that in reference to one who *wants* to change his own *middos*. How much more difficult is it, therefore, for someone who wants to change someone else's *middos*, even if that someone else is their child.

But don't parents have an obligation to be *mechaneich* their children?!

Absolutely! *Chinuch habanim*, however, does not require parents to attempt to break their children's *middos*. Rather, they should guide their children by teaching and helping their children to adopt proper *middos*.

One of the biggest mistakes, therefore, that parents make is trying to crush a child's natural temperament. For example, in the situation you described, some parents would feel that it is their duty to punish a child who would insist on having a whole portion of ices when everyone else was getting only a half. They would feel that such poor *middos* must be stamped out with whatever force is necessary. These parenting tactics never accomplish positive results and only lead to creating many more problems down the road.

If parents are not supposed to punish their children for bad *middos*, then how are they supposed to be *mechaneich* their children?

Parents can teach proper *middos* in two ways. The first is by example. It is the most effective method and also the least often utilized by many parents. For example, your wife taught good *middos* in the episode you reported by speaking "calmly" to your son. Too often parents explode in anger when their children misbehave, setting a perfect example of poor *middos*. As the Ramban wrote at the beginning of his famous *igeres* to his son, "Accustom yourself always to say everything calmly to everyone at all times. And through this you will be saved from anger which is a bad *middah* causing people to sin."

The second way to teach proper *middos* is to demonstrate to children that faulty *middos* lead to negative consequences. Once again, your wife hit the bull's-eye when she informed your son that the only alternative to half an ice was none at all. Suffering the deprivation of ices will eventually teach your son that flexibility and compromise can bring its own rewards.

You and your wife are questioning whether she should have "given in" and let your son have a whole one. Perhaps you are wondering whether she was being stubborn. To have given in to his demand, however, would have been a serious mistake. That would have taught him the wrong lesson. It would have taught him that intransigence pays off. And it would have planted the seeds for the next battle when he would attempt to repeat his "success."

Finally, the best advice I can give you for dealing with such a child is to learn to see this issue in a broader, long-term perspective. It is certainly frustrating when you are seated around the Shabbos table serving dessert and the tranquility is disturbed by the persistent demands of your obstinate 13-year-old. You should bear in mind, however, that there is a positive side to your son's tenaciousness. It can, at times, lead to major success in life.

Take a look at those people in your community whom you consider to be successful. Whether it is the respected *lamdan* and rosh hayeshivah or even the prominent professional and wealthy businessman, what they all have in common is their unrelenting drive to achieve their goals.

A wise man once said, "Success is 1 percent inspiration and 99 percent perspiration." In order to work hard, overcome obstacles and accomplish great feats, one must be able to remain focused on his or her goal without letting go.

The Ponevezher Rav, *ztz"l*, was determined to rebuild his yeshivah in Bnei Brak after World War II. It seemed at the time like an impossible task. He was quoted as having said, "People say I am dreaming. It may be so. But at least I am not sleeping."

We all want our children to be successful in life. The same trait that troubles you now may very well prove to be an asset to your son as he matures and develops. Instead of trying to make him into someone else, your responsibility as a parent is to help him become all that he can be. And having a little stubbornness in him could end up going a long way toward helping him achieve that goal.

What Do I Tell My Two Teenage Daughters When They Ask Me Where I Am Going and I Don't Want Them to Know?

Every so often, I run into a predicament with my two teenage daughters, ages 15 and 17. If I have to leave the house and I do not want them to know where I am going, they pepper me with questions: "Where are you going?" "Why are you in such a hurry?" "How come you can't tell us?" "What's the big secret?" You get the idea.

If I tell them that I have to meet with someone, they insist on knowing who it is and what it's all about. If I tell them firmly that it does not have anything to do with them, they ask, "Why are you mad at us?"

I'm sure that I'm not the only mother of teenage daughters who goes through this. But I suspect that there may be a better way of handling this. As the situation stands now, I begin feeling stressed out as soon as I realize that I will have to go out somewhere private while they will be at home.

They both have day camp jobs this summer which means they will be at home much more than during the school year. So I really could use some tips now on how to deal with this issue more effectively.

As Avraham Avinu and Yitzchak Avinu were ascending Har HaMoriah for the *akeidah*, Yitzchak asked his father, "Where is the lamb for the sacrifice?" (*Bereishis* 22:7). Avraham replied somewhat enigmatically that Hashem will identify the offering (ibid. v. 8). On this latter *pasuk*, Harav Shimshon Rephael Hirsch, *ztz"l*, commented, "And with that Avraham had told him everything that he had to know, which he needed to know."

In this case, of course, Yitzchak understood much more than he was told. He understood that he was to be the offering. In your case, however, your daughters do not know where you are going unless you share that information with them. The point here is that similar to Avraham and Yitzchak, you only have to tell your daughters that which they "need to know."

Children are allowed, and often encouraged, to ask their parents questions. It is only by asking that children can learn all that which they need to know. As it says in *Pirkei Avos* (2:5), "A shy person cannot learn." And on this *mishnah* the Tiferes Yisrael comments, "Because he is apprehensive that people will view him as uninformed, he remains chronically uninformed."

As we see from Avraham Avinu's example, however, parents are not required to answer each of their children's questions with all the information they are seeking. As Harav Hirsch implies, parents should only provide the information that the children need to know. Not more and not less.

It is quite common for children to be curious about their parents. This is not at all unhealthy. In fact, it contributes to the natural process of identity development for children to know more rather than less about their parents.

Children of all ages, for example, love to hear stories about their parents when they were children. If you ever want to grab your children's attention — at any time, for any reason — just offer to relate an episode they have not yet heard from your past. Then watch how quickly they stop whatever they were doing and become attentive listeners.

Children are also extremely curious about the private lives of their parents, where they go, what they do, and with whom they do it. Just because they are curious about these matters, however, does not mean that parents must satisfy their children's curiosity at all times. In fact, it is even healthy for children to be frustrated in their attempts to uncover their parents' secrets for two reasons.

First, it is important for children to learn — and this lesson can never be reinforced enough — that families are not democracies. Not all family members have equal rights, privileges, and responsibilities.

For example, parents have the right and responsibility to know where their children are at all times. As children grow up and mature, however, they need to be granted more and more independence. So while parents may know the exact location of their 6-year-old at all times, a 16-year-old may be granted greater latitude by virtue of his or her greater sense of accountability and the trust earned by past performance.

Children, on the other hand, do not have the same right to know where their parents are at all times. Even though they might like to have this information, it is not necessary for them to know. If, however, parents grant their children access to this information, they are acting in a way that family therapists call, "blurring the generational boundaries of the family."

What that means is that each generation in a family has its own rights and obligations. What applies to grandparents does not apply to parents. What is appropriate for parents is not necessarily appropriate for children. When parents treat children as if they were on equal footing with the parents, they are investing too much power in the children and not setting proper limits, and this is unhealthy for everyone.

I recall, for example, one 8-year-old boy who had a host of psychological problems. He was often sad, had difficulty making friends, preferred to play with younger children, and acted out in school. His intelligence, however, was above average. And there did not appear to be any explanation for his social immaturity until I learned that he had complete free access to his parents' bedroom! In fact, he left his own room a few nights every week to sleep with his parents due to his "night fears."

When I explained to his parents the importance of maintaining proper boundaries, they confessed that they realized the free access to their bedroom was not good for him. Nevertheless, they felt helpless to change his behavior. They then agreed to follow my directions for keeping him out of their room at night. And they were pleasantly surprised to see that their son's problems dissipated as soon as they succeeded in enforcing the "off-limits" policy regarding their bedroom.

The second reason it is beneficial for children to be frustrated in their attempts to obtain private information about their parents is because it sets the proper example. When these children grow up and become parents themselves, it will be too late to teach them about maintaining proper generational boundaries. The best way for them to learn how to set the right tone after marriage is for them to observe it while they are growing up.

Returning to your original question, I would suggest you say all or part of the following. "I do not mind your asking. And I am certainly not angry with you for asking. But I do not feel that it is necessary for you to know where I am going right now. Sometimes I do tell you where I am going. Other times, however, I prefer not to share that information with you. And this is one of those times. I'll see you later, *iy"H*."

My 12-Year-Old Stepdaughter Will Be Visiting Her Biological Father Who Is No Longer Frum

My wife and I have been happily married for nine years. This is a second marriage for both of us. I have two children from my first marriage who live with their mother. My wife has one child, a 12-year-old daughter from her first marriage, who lives with us. And we have two children together: an 8-year-old boy and a 5-year-old girl.

My wife and her first husband divorced almost 11 years ago, shortly after their daughter was born. The primary reason for this was that her ex decided that he no longer wanted to remain *frum*. He adopted a completely secular lifestyle and moved to Florida.

The divorce papers stipulated that my wife would be allowed to make all educational decisions for her daughter unilaterally. And, so far, her ex has been supportive and cooperative of our sending her daughter to a regular Bais Yaakov here in New York. The only problem, however, is that the court also granted him two weeks of visitation every summer, during which he is allowed to bring her to Florida.

As far as we can tell, he has kept his word to give her only kosher food and not to make her be *mechaleil* Shabbos. Of course, his definitions of that may differ from ours. Nevertheless, this arrangement has more or less worked out because we relied on the leniency that our daughter was still a *ketanah*, a minor.

This year, however, she had her *bas mitzvah*. So this summer is the first time she will be going to Florida as a *gedolah*. That, coupled with the fact that she is becoming more independent (and even a bit rebellious, lately), is causing us to be more anxious about her spending so much time with her non*frum* father.

We have already consulted with a top matrimonial lawyer

who discouraged us from trying to go to court to reduce the summer visitation schedule. So that is not an option. Is there anything else we can do, therefore, to protect our preteenage daughter from being drawn away, *chas v'shalom*, from *Yiddishkeit* when she goes to Florida again this summer?

**At the end** of *Birchos Hashachar*, we recite two *tefillos*, both beginning, "*V'yehi ratzon mil'fanecha . . .*," asking Hashem to protect us from a long list of spiritual and physical dangers. There is only one item that is repeated in both *tefillos*: *chaver ra*, a bad friend. Apparently, *Chazal* felt that the potential danger is so great that we must beseech Hashem to shield us from a *chaver ra* twice every morning.

Furthermore, *Chazal* teach, "*Harcheik me'shachein ra*, distance yourself from a bad neighbor" (*Pirkei Avos* 1:7). On this *mishnah* the *Bartenura* comments, "In order that you not learn from his ways."

As parents, therefore, you are justified in being concerned about the potentially negative influences on your daughter's *Yiddishkeit* by people whom she befriends. Unfortunately, however, children cannot choose their biological parents. And you are unable to restrict her contact with her non*frum* father. So what can you do to protect her?

As you live in New York, you may be familiar with the Bronx Zoo. A few years ago, on a *Chol HaMoed* trip with my family, I visited the aviary there. I was fascinated by the fact that there appeared to be no fences, screens or glass partitions between the birds and the visitors.

To satisfy my curiosity, I asked one of the staff about this. He explained that my perception was accurate. There was nothing separating the birds from the visitors. Why then, I asked, do the birds not fly out into the corridors and disturb the people? What keeps them inside their individual habitats?

The zookeeper then explained to me that each one of the natural habitats contains all of the food and water that the birds could ever want. In addition, the darkened hallways and the well-lit habitats create the illusion of a black wall for the birds. "Since they have everything they could possibly want inside, there is no reason for them to even think of venturing outside," he said.

Your task, therefore, is to deal with your daughter in the same way. You must do everything you can to make a Torah lifestyle so appealing and pleasant for her that she will have no desire to "venture outside."

In order to achieve this goal, it is not necessary for you to give in to her every wish and whim. It is vital, however, for you to make sure that she is happy and satisfied.

If your daughter has recently displayed some rebelliousness, for example, as you indicate in your letter, then that may be a signal that something is bothering her. If so, that most definitely should not be ignored. Rebelliousness in preadolescents is a red flag that parents must take seriously.

This may be your daughter's way of trying to communicate her displeasure or disappointment with something going on at home. You really need to get to the bottom of this. And it certainly would be advisable to do so now, before the summer.

Sit down with her and have a heart-to-heart talk. Ask her if anything is bothering her about the way you and your wife are treating her. If she denies that anything is wrong, do not sigh with relief. If she has been rebellious lately, most likely there is something upsetting her. If she denies that there is, that may only be because she is not ready to talk about it.

Ask her *if* something bothered her, would she feel comfortable telling you? If she hesitates even slightly, take that as a sign that she would not. Then ask her what you do or don't do that would make it difficult for her to tell you what is bothering her.

Should you not get anywhere with this line of questioning, then you might want to consider getting some professional help. A trained family therapist may be needed to facilitate this important communication between you and your daughter. In the safety of a therapist's office, your daughter may be willing to open up and tell you what is bothering her. Then, and only then, will you be able to address the issue and make whatever adjustments are needed at home to make her feel more comfortable. And once she feels more comfortable at home, she will no longer need to act out her feelings with rebellious behavior.

When you ask your daughter if anything is bothering her, it is entirely possible that she will tell you. She may complain, for example, that you are too strict with her and do not let her do this or that. Her accusations may be valid or they may be somewhat exaggerated or distorted in some way. In either case, you must not dismiss her feelings. Try to first reflect or repeat in your own words what she is telling you. That way, you will be sure you understand her and she will feel heard. Only then should you try to resolve her complaints through compromise. If this is not possible, then you may still need to meet with a therapist who can guide you all to a workable solution to the conflict.

Twelve-year-olds, of course, can be upset about other relationships besides their parents. For example, a 12-year-old can feel devastated if a formerly close friend recently rejected her or him. (S)he can also feel very down if a teacher has harshly rebuked her or him. And (s)he can be very unhappy if (s)he was publicly humiliated, in any way.

In your daughter's case, however, I do not suspect that she is unhappy about any nonfamilial relationship. Twelve-year-olds do not respond to social injuries by becoming more rebellious. They do respond to conflicts with their parents, however, by becoming more rebellious. For that reason, therefore, I suspect that what is bothering your daughter has to do with you and your wife and not any other significant person in her life.

As Dr. David Pelcovitz once put it, "Rules without relationships provoke rebellion" (*Kids of Hope*, Hamodia Special Supplement, Pesach 5770, p. 37). I am not suggesting here that you have no relationship, *chas v'shalom*, with your daughter. Rather, I am simply pointing out that if your daughter has become "a bit rebellious lately" then you may need help in strengthening some aspect of your relationship with her.

Finally, once you have straightened out whatever is causing her to be rebellious recently, you will feel more secure about her commitment to *Yiddishkeit* and she will be better protected from any potentially negative influences from her father this summer.

Isn't Rebelliousness in Adolescents a Sign That They Are Normal?

I would like to comment on your column, "My 12-Year-Old Stepdaughter Will Be Visiting Her Biological Father Who Is No Longer *Frum*."

While I admire and appreciate the *mashal* you gave about a bird who has all of its needs satisfied, and so does not fly away, I do not understand these words: "If your daughter has recently displayed some rebelliousness, that may be a signal that something is bothering her. It should not be ignored. Rebelliousness in adolescents is a red flag for parents."

Isn't rebelliousness in adolescents a sign that they are normal? It is our job as parents to be there for them, to help them, to love them, to listen to them, and — perhaps most of all — to set limits and stay firm, with an attitude of *gam zeh yaavor*. But I do not feel that rebelliousness alone is a reason to take a child to a therapist.

Teens and preteens, especially if they are female, may tend to prefer talking with their friends or their mothers rather than their stepfathers. This too is normal. Perhaps hesitancy to confide in a stepfather is not a reason to take a child to a therapist.

Rebelliousness among adolescents is extremely common. I would not go as far as to say, however, that it is "a sign that they are normal." If that were so, then any adolescent who is *not* rebellious would have to be considered "abnormal." And that is certainly not the case. There are many, many adolescents who are not at all rebellious and they are still quite healthy, well adjusted, and normal.

Adolescents may, and often do, test the limits set by their parents. They will attempt to see just how far they can go before their behavior triggers a negative consequence. This form of testing is extremely normal and should not be confused with the more confrontational and openly defiant behavior which constitutes rebelliousness.

I would agree with you that the job of parents is to be there for their children, "to help them, to love them, to listen to them," and to set limits for them. I am not sure what you mean, however, by "an attitude of *gam zeh yaavor*." If you meant that parents should not overreact to their children's misbehavior, including rebelliousness, then I heartily agree with you. If, however, you meant that parents should look away and disregard the clear warning signals that something is bothering their children, then I vehemently disagree.

When I wrote that rebelliousness should not be ignored, what I meant was that parents must learn to see all misbehavior — including rebelliousness — as a sign that something is bothering the child.

The story is told of a young orphan boy who was drawn to the shul where the Baal Shem Tov was davening on Rosh Hashanah. Standing in the back, the uneducated boy observed the inspiring *tefillos*. Overcome with emotion, he yearned to participate. Finally, he took out a whistle and blew it loudly. All of the *mispallelim* stopped, turned, and glared at the boy, while some began to rebuke him.

The Baal Shem Tov ran over to defend the boy and declared, "Does not Dovid HaMelech say, '*Karov Hashem l'chol kor'av l'chol asher yik'ro'uhu b'emes*, Hashem is close to all those who call upon Him, to all who call upon Him sincerely' (*Tehillim* 145:18). Who is to say whether our *shofar*-blowing today was more sincere than this boy's whistling?"

Similarly, rebelliousness in adolescents represents the behavioral expression of feelings that they cannot communicate verbally. If parents ignore it, it will not simply go away. On the contrary, it is most likely to intensify.

For that reason, when parents see rebelliousness in their adolescent children, they need find out what is prompting that behavior. What is it that has so upset this child?

The best method for discovering what is bothering an adolescent is to talk with him or her. As I recommended in that column, parents must sit down and have a heart-to-heart talk with their child. When feelings are expressed verbally, it is no longer necessary to act them out. I fully agree with you, therefore, that "rebelliousness alone is not a reason to take a child to a therapist." But rebelliousness alone is a reason to sit down and try to talk with a child. And that is what I meant by a red flag.

If parents try to communicate with their adolescent child and do not get anywhere, however, then they may need to seek professional help. Open communication is essential to maintain healthy family life. As long as parents and children can talk about the things that bother each of them, they can eventually solve whatever problems present themselves. If, however, the lines of communication break down and children cannot or will not speak with their parents. then parents must not neglect that danger sign.

I also agree with you that "teens and preteens, especially girls, may tend to prefer talking with their friends or their mothers rather than their stepfathers." That is certainly not a cause for alarm.

If, however, the teens and preteens are acting rebelliously at home — regardless of their gender — both parents need to speak with them about what is going on. They need to encourage open expression of whatever is bothering their children about the way they are being treated at home. Instead of seeing the rebellious behavior as normal and ignoring it, the parents must see it as a warning signal that something is wrong at home that must be fixed.

No child should be forced to confide in any parent, whether stepparent or biological. Children must be allowed to choose in whom they wish to confide, just as adults do. But if children do not confide in either parent and they are dealing with a problem that originates outside of the home, then the fact that they cannot discuss it at home becomes a major part of the problem that needs to be fixed.

If a child is acting out his or her angry feelings toward a parent by behaving in a rebellious fashion, however, then being asked to talk about it would not violate what was stated above.

In the case presented in the original letter, the 12-year-old girl has been living with her mother and stepfather for the past nine years. If she is unhappy at home, for any reason, and that is prompting her to behave in a rebellious fashion, then for her parents to see her unwillingness to talk to her stepfather about her feelings as "normal" and "not a reason to" go for help would be a dereliction of their responsibility as parents.

If, on the other hand, this girl would have opened up to her mother and confided in her, then we can assume the matter would have been resolved and the stepfather would not have needed to mention it in his letter. Clearly, then, this was a girl who had difficulty communicating with *both* parents and that is why I recommended that if attempts to communicate with her did not bear fruit, family therapy designed to facilitate the communication should be considered.

Finally, let me clarify that my answers are written to respond to the specific cases presented and based on the personal information provided in each letter. Hopefully, other readers may glean insights and practical parenting strategies from my answers. But they were never intended to represent the final word on any given subject in every situation.

From your letter, you sound like a parent who assumes a more laid-back position with your children which is certainly legitimate and, in many cases, helpful. Parents who do not get bent out of shape, roll with the punches, and adopt an attitude of *gam zeh ya'avor* (This, too, shall pass) generally avoid the common yet serious trap of overreacting to their children's misdeeds. And that is certainly a good thing. So, if my assessment of your parenting style is accurate, then your children are fortunate that you are their parent.

Our 17-Year-Old Son Prefers a "Learning-Only" Yeshivah, While I Believe He Should Attend One That Allows Part-Time College

Our 17-year-old son is graduating high school and will be moving on to *yeshivah gedolah* after the summer.

So far, he has not expressed strong feelings about any particular yeshivah. He has indicated, however, that he would prefer to attend a "learning-only" type of yeshivah.

I am very opposed to my son's plans, as I am looking out for his long-term interests. In order to eventually be able to earn a livelihood and support a family, therefore, I believe he should attend a yeshivah that allows part-time college together with the Torah learning. My wife hears where each of us is coming from and doesn't have strong feelings about this issue.

So far, I have avoided a full "knock-down, drag-out" discussion with my son on this matter. He has not brought it up and neither have I. But he will have to make a final decision shortly. Before I sit down with him to discuss this I wanted to get some input from you as to how you feel I should be handling this conversation.

Basically, you have three options here. You could say nothing and let him make this decision completely on his own. You could force him to do what you think is in his best interest. Or, you could share your point of view with him, stopping short of pressuring him to follow your direction. Let us look at each choice separately.

If you say nothing at all, you avoid any conflict or confrontation, which is good. On the other hand, you may give the impression that you either do not care what he does or that this decision is not an important one. As neither of those are messages you would ever want to send, you can now rule out the first option.

If you coerce your son to go to the yeshivah that will allow part-time college study, you may very well succeed in getting him to attend. Your success, however, may be short lived. Just because he attends that yeshivah together with college will not insure that he will flourish at either learning program. There is, however, a good chance he will fail at either or both. And here is why.

All 17-year-olds believe in their heart of hearts that they are smarter than their parents. Even if they do not admit it, it goes with the territory of being an older adolescent.

Mark Twain supposedly once said, "When I was 16, I thought my father was so stupid I could hardly bear to have the old man around. When I was 20, I was surprised how much he had learned in four years!"

By compelling your son to learn where you prefer, you are saying, "I know better than you what is good for you. If you follow my plan, eventually you will see that I was right."

Once you have adopted that position, your son has a very easy way to prove that you were wrong: failing. But why would he want to fail? you might ask. Everyone prefers success over failure.

For the most part, that is true. One major exception to that rule, however, is the adolescent. Proving his parents wrong and himself right is so important to some adolescents that they may even be willing to harm themselves. The incentive of vanquishing the parents is so great that an adolescent may — as the saying goes – cut off his nose to spite his face.

Even if an adolescent is not invested in proving his parents wrong, there is another reason why coercion is not a recommended parenting strategy. Coercion interferes with the development of self-motivation.

One of the chief complaints parents express about their adolescent and young-adult children is that they are not motivated. They are seen as lazy, lacking energy, and drive to accomplish and be productive. "When I was his age," these parents gripe, "I worked and/or studied so hard that I am exhausted now just remembering how busy I was then!"

These parents often fail to recognize their own role in crushing their child's natural motivation. All children are born with a will to accomplish. Just look at how busy a 2-year-old is all day and you will understand how every child begins life with this natural drive to achieve.

However, when parents totally ignore the child's feelings and repeatedly impose their will on the child, the child learns some unfortunate lessons. He learns that his feelings are not important. He learns that his preferences do not count. And he learns that it does not pay to get enthusiastic about any project because his parents will be imposing their will on him anyway. *So why bother?* he thinks to himself. After years of this approach a child's normal motivation will have been effectively pulverized to the point of nonexistence.

If, on the other hand, you encourage your child to pursue *his* goals and learn in the yeshivah of *his* choice, then you will be enhancing his motivation and fostering the ideal conditions for him to succeed. Bolstered with your support, he stands the greatest chance of becoming as productive as he can be.

If you are not yet convinced that the third option listed above is the one you should choose, listen to the words of *Chazal*. "A person should only learn Torah in the place that he desires. As it says [*Tehillim* 2:2], '. . . only the Torah of Hashem that he desires'" (*Avodah Zarah* 19a). And on this *Gemara* Rashi comments, "His *rebbi* should only teach him the *mesechta* that he requests because if he teaches him another *mesechta*, he will not succeed since his mind [will only focus] on [that which] he desires."

Hopefully, you will heed the words of *Chazal* and not attempt to impose your will on your son. Of course, that does not preclude your sharing your opinion. But this should be done in a tone which does not imply that your judgment is inherently superior to his.

You should not begin, therefore, by saying, "If you're smart, you'll go to yeshivah _____." Instead, you should present your ideas as just another piece of information he can take onto his plate along with many others available to him from the smorgasbord of life. For example, you might present your thoughts this way.

"Before you make up your mind as to which yeshivah you will attend next year, I wanted to share with you some of my thoughts. I think yeshivah _____ would be best for you for the following reasons. Certainly, the final decision is up to you. And I wish you much *hatzlachah* wherever you finally decide to learn."

Finally, you must steer clear of the common parenting pitfall of assuming that decisions made by a 17-year-old are etched in stone. At 17, a young person is still experimenting. The choices he or she makes, whether positive or negative, do not necessarily chart the course for the rest of their lives.

If you believe your son should attend a yeshivah that allows part-time college because of your concerns about *parnassah,* you could reopen the discussion of this subject with him in a year or two. At that time, he may be more receptive to your way of thinking. Or, you may be so impressed with his dedication to learning that you will be more in sync with his goals in life.

My point here is simply that a lot can change in a year or two. And you should not see the choice of yeshivah for your son for next year as a point of no return.

At Home, My 15-Year-Old Daughter Has a Short Fuse

I think my 15-year-old daughter may need anger management. She is our youngest child and has just completed tenth grade. Academically, she is an above-average student who works hard to maintain her grades. Socially, she is quite popular and seems to be friendly with most of her classmates. She is also very talented in music and dance. And, consequently, she is always extremely active in planning and participating in all sorts of performances at school and camp. In short, she is a well-rounded girl from whom I *schep* a lot of *nachas*.

The one area, however, which causes me a great deal of concern is her temper. It does not seem to be a major issue between her and her friends. But she does flare up often at home with me and, to a lesser extent, with my husband.

Let me give you two recent examples. My daughter came home from school recently and complained about a conversation she had with one of her classmates. In that conversation, she felt that the other girl was unfairly pressuring her to accept too much responsibility for a joint assignment. When I tried to explain to her what she could have said to that girl to get her to back off, she blew up at me.

On another occasion, my daughter was worrying about a test she had just taken. She compared notes with classmates after the exam and feared that she may have failed. I tried to comfort her and make her feel better by offering suggestions. In response, my daughter ridiculed my suggestions and became infuriated, running up to her room in tears.

What can I do to help my daughter learn to control her temper?

**If you told me** that your daughter gets angry with her friends, her siblings, and both of her parents, I would agree with you that she needs help in learning to control her temper. Since her outbursts occur primarily with you, however, we have to suspect that they are being triggered by something in your relationship with her.

Your daughter comes home feeling frustrated, disappointed or upset by some unpleasant event during the day. She turns to you, her mother, for sympathy and support. That is a normal, typical, and appropriate thing for a 15-year-old girl to do.

Instead of giving her the commiseration she is seeking, you attempt to solve her problems by offering solutions. What, you may ask, is wrong with that? In a word, plenty.

Regardless of how brilliant, correct or helpful the suggestions may be, solutions add fuel to the fire for a number of reasons. First, suggestions are a subtle form of criticism. They carry the (albeit unintended) message, "If you had done things the right way, you would not have gotten yourself into this mess in the first place."

In addition, suggestions can be heard as put-downs. Some people can hear within them the unspoken message, "I am so much smarter than you. I know so much more than you. In fact, I know how to solve your problems even if you do not."

Moreover, attempts to fix the problems can be seen as intolerance of the sufferer's feelings. It is as if the helper were saying, "I cannot stand to listen to you vent such emotions. Take my advice now so I will not have to deal with your feelings anymore." This could leave the complainer feeling lost, alone, and abandoned.

Finally, when the listener focuses on solving the problem *exclusively*, the sufferer can feel that the listener cares more about the problem than about the sufferer. Many times people want and need understanding more than solutions that may not be realistic or helpful anyway. It is, in part, for that reason that people are willing to pay large sums of money to psychotherapists for the opportunity to speak with someone who will understand and empathize, even if no advice is dispensed.

Chazal, of course, understood all of this well before the word psychology was even invented. As they taught, "Do not [even attempt] to appease your friend while he is [still] angry" (*Pirkei Avos* 4:18). On this *mishnah*, *Rashi* explains that it "will not help you." Rabbeinu Yonah and the Tiferes Yisrael both comment that it "will only intensify his anger."

All of this is not to imply that parents should never give advice to their children. Advising children is one of the most valuable gifts parents can provide. But there is a time and place for everything. When children solicit advice, that is the optimum time to provide it. When they are upset, frustrated or angry, however, that is the worst time to dispense suggestions.

Returning to your daughter, she may not be in need of anger management. What she might need, however, is a mother who knows how to listen effectively by responding empathically. I certainly never condone disrespect toward parents. But what you see as her short fuse could possibly be her frustration with your misunderstanding of her needs. When she complains to you, she may not be asking for solutions or advice. She may be simply trying to solicit your sympathy and understanding.

If so, what is the correct way to respond empathically? Just acknowledge her feelings. Articulate and label them for her if she cannot do so for herself. Say things such as, "You were annoyed at her because you thought she was trying to dump more work on you"; or, "You worked so hard studying and now you think you did not do as well on the test as you had hoped. You are very disappointed."

If your daughter says, "No. That is not how I feel!" then ask her to correct you. And try again until you get it right.

If your daughter says, "Yes. That's exactly how I feel," then just sit there with her. Your caring, silent presence can be more comforting than words, as we learn from the friends of Iyov who came from so far to comfort him. Yet, when they arrived, they said nothing. "And they sat with him on the ground for seven days and seven nights. And they did not say anything to him because they saw how great was his pain" (*Iyov* 2:13).

Recently, an *almanah* confided to me that she feels very frustrated when she complains to her friends and they offer advice. "Since I do not have a husband now, sometimes I just need someone to listen to me," she said, hoping at least I would understand. And I did. So I nodded and said nothing.

Our 13-Year-Old Feels Dominated by His Same-Age Cousin

I need some advice regarding a situation that we will be confronted with over *Yom Tov, iy"H.*

My married brother lives out of town. As a result, the only time I get to see him, aside from *simchahs*, is during *Yom Tov,* when he comes with his family and stays with our parents who live on the next street. He and his family usually come to us for a meal. And we go to my parents for at least one meal so we can spend as much time together as possible over *Yom Tov.*

I very much look forward to these reunions because I have a good relationship with my brother and sister-in-law. Unfortunately, my 13-year-old son does not get along with his first cousin who is the same age.

We have an older daughter, who is 16, and two younger daughters, ages 4 and 6. My brother has five children, two girls, ages 17 and 18, and three boys, ages 5, 7, and 13. Consequently, whenever we get together with his family, the older girls go off together to talk, the younger kids sit down to play, and the two 13-year-olds are paired off by default.

My nephew is a fine *bachur*, although he is a bit strong willed and tends to dominate whatever game he plays. Our 13-year-old is somewhat more *eidel* (gentle) and does not speak up for himself as much as he should. In fact, I was completely unaware that he did not get along well with his cousin until last week. He overheard me speaking to my brother about getting together over *Yom Tov* and maybe even one day on *Chol Hamoed.* When I got off the phone, my son blurted out how much he can't stand spending time with his cousin.

Now I feel torn between my desire to visit with my brother and my son's wish to avoid his cousin. What would you recommend?

There are long-term and short-term solutions to your dilemma. As far as this upcoming *Yom Tov* is concerned, there is no reason your 13-year-old son has to be committed to visiting with his cousin for the full amount of time you are spending with your brother. He is entitled, for example, to have other "plans" to get together with friends.

More specifically, you should tell your son that he can arrange to meet a friend after each *Yom Tov* meal at which your family and your brother's family will be eating together. Then you can inform your brother the next time you speak with him that you are looking forward to the reunion. You would also like him to let his son know, however, that your son will be going to learn with a *chavrusa* after the meal.

If your son does not feel trapped into spending many hours with a cousin whose company he does not enjoy, he may be much less resentful of your family reunions.

On a more long-term basis, however, what you need to work on with your son is teaching him how to be more assertive. Apparently, your son finds it difficult to achieve a greater comfort level with his cousin whom you describe as more "strong willed."

The Torah records the content of a critical communication between Dovid HaMelech and his 12-year-old son, Shlomo, shortly after Shlomo had been anointed king. "Strengthen yourself and become a man" (*II Melachim* 2:2). And as the *Metzudas Dovid* explains, Dovid HaMelech was telling his son, "Even though you are still only a lad, strengthen yourself as if you were a fully matured adult."

Similarly, you need to teach your son — who happens to be not much older than Shlomo HaMelech was when his father spoke the inspiring words quoted above — that it is a vital social skill to be able to tell others what they are doing that makes him uncomfortable. If, for example, his cousin is dominating the conversation or the time they spend together, your son must develop the confidence to speak up for himself.

You can begin this project by asking your son what he would like, someday, to be able to tell his cousin. Get him to verbalize his feelings to you.

Next, you can validate those feelings. Tell your son that you would feel the same way if another adult treated you as your nephew treats your son.

Point out to him that his reaction to his cousin's objectionable behavior is perfectly legitimate.

Then explore with your son why he feels he could not actually say those things directly to his cousin. What is he afraid of? What negative consequences does he anticipate? Go through each item separately. Assess together how likely each one is to occur. And suggest effective strategies to your son for dealing with each contingency about which he is apprehensive.

Finally, offer to role-play the confrontation with him. Start by letting him play the role of his cousin and you play the role of your son. Let him act out the offensive or irritating comments. Then you respond as your son stated he would like to be able to do. Then reverse the roles with you playing your nephew and your son playing himself. For example, if your nephew always insists on playing the game he chooses, pretend you are your son and say, "Last time we played the game you wanted. How about letting me choose this time?"

Your son may interrupt the role-play, saying he just does not believe he can do it. Do not argue or debate him on this point. That would not be helpful. Instead, pursue his resistance. Ask him why he feels pessimistic. Go back and review his worst-case scenario and offer him advice on how to encourage and reassure himself. When you are finished, invite him again to engage in the role-play with you.

If your son is still resistant, do not push the matter any further, for that day. A day or two later, however, revisit the topic and the invitation to engage in the role-play. By respecting his anxious feelings without surrendering to them, you will be helping your son to whittle away at them until he will be able to complete the role-play.

Once your son has completed the role-play with you, ask him how ready he feels to implement the strategy. If he tells you he is not ready yet, do not push him. Simply repeat the role-play another day and keep repeating it until your son feels confident.

Eventually, your son will confront his cousin. If your son is successful, it may actually improve the relationship between the two boys. If he is unsuccessful, however, this need not be viewed as a failure by you or your son. It should be seen only as an indication that a bit more work is needed to revise the plan or its implementation. Do not give up and do not allow your son to be discouraged. Return to the steps outlined above and keep at it until your son develops the confidence he needs.

Finally, bear in mind that your son may never be able to be more assertive with this particular cousin. After all, it is not a *shidduch* where incompatibilities must be resolved at all costs. The social skill of assertiveness, however, is one which your son will need to master in order to succeed in life. And whatever you can do now to help him achieve it will stand him in good stead for the future in dealing with other strong-willed people.

We Need Guidelines for Establishing Parameters for Our Children's Relationships With Our Secular Relatives

I am concerned about the relationship our family has with my wife's secular relatives. My wife and I are *ba'alei teshuvah*. We now live in a *charedi* community in the Jerusalem area. We have a 16-year-old boy and four girls ranging from age 15 to age 9. The relatives recently visited us on Succos and were here for five hours. My son spent a couple of hours effectively defending living a Torah life to his 25-year-old female cousin. This could have positive effects but I am sure he encountered concepts that he never heard before and I do not know if he was able to answer all of her questions. In addition, I am extremely uncomfortable with him having even a five-minute semi-private conversation with an unmarried, attractive female who lives a very secular life.

On the other side of the *succah*, my 15-year-old daughter asked me if she could meet her aunt for lunch in some secular city in Israel. I gave her a look of astonishment and think she got the message. Other nerve-racking incidents were taking place at the table, but I think you have the idea.

It is important for my wife to maintain a close and warm relationship with her secular family, but we need to know what parameters must be set for us to give our children the best chance to stay *frum*.

Baruch Hashem, my wife has agreed to no longer visit her secular relatives at their homes, which is not easy for her. My feeling is that the closer the children feel to the secular relatives, the more we are creating for them a confusing perspective of their own *hashkafah*, *chas v'shalom*.

What guidelines can you give us for what I am sure is a common problem?

**Whenever questions** of *hashkafah* are raised, it is always necessary to turn to primary Torah sources for guidance.

In *Parashas Vayishlach* (*Bereishis* 32:23), The Torah tells us, "And he [Yaakov Avinu] got up that night [before his confrontation with Eisav] and he took his two wives and his two concubines and his eleven children and he crossed [the Jordan River at the] Yabok Crossing."

Rashi asks, "And where was [his 12th child] Dinah?" He answers by quoting the *midrash*, that Yaakov Avinu locked her up in a chest to protect her from Eisav. And for this he was punished.

In order to gain greater clarity on this puzzling *midrash*, it is necessary to quote it in its entirety (*Bereishis Rabbah* 76:9). "He [Yaakov Avinu] put her [Dinah] in a chest and locked her up. He said, 'This wicked man [Eisav] is not at all on her [spiritual] level. [I have locked up Dinah] so that he [Eisav] should not see her and take her from me [as a wife].' Rav Huna in the name of Rav Abba HaKohen Bardula said: *HaKadosh Baruch Hu* said: 'One who withholds kindness from his friend' (*Iyov* 6:14) [refers to you, Yaakov]. You have withheld kindness from your brother [Eisav]. Had you married [Dinah to Eisav], she would not have been violated [by Sh'chem]. You did not seek to have her marry one who was circumcised and behold she married one who was uncircumcised. You did not seek to have her cohabit in a permitted fashion and behold she cohabited in a prohibited fashion."

How are we to understand this *midrash*? Certainly it cannot be seen as an injunction to abandon our responsibilities to safeguard our children's *Yiddishkeit*!

The *ba'alei mussar* suggest that Yaakov Avinu was totally justified in taking such extreme measures to protect Dinah from marrying Eisav. If so, then why was he deserving of punishment? They answer that as he was locking the chest, he failed to feel sufficient pain for his brother. He focused on his own needs to save Dinah and did not empathize enough with the plight of Eisav.

In more practical terms, therefore, you are not meant to sacrifice your children's spiritual safety in order to help bring your secular relatives closer to Torah. On the other hand, however, you are also not free to totally abandon these not-yet-*frum* relatives.

Hillel told the prospective *ger* that the entire Torah can be summed up by the statement, "What is hateful to you, do not do to your fellow" (*Shabbos* 31a). How do we see the laws of *tefillin*, *kashrus*, and Shabbos included in that statement? The answer is that since the Torah way of life is the ideal, the opposite is abhorrent. You should be unable, therefore, to sit by and tolerate a fellow Jew living a secular life without your attempting to influence him. We all have a responsibility to reach out to be *m'kareiv* our fellow Jews who are not yet *frum*. But we clearly have a *greater* responsibility to reach out to those not-yet-*frum* Jews who live next door, work across the hall or are members of our family.

When distributing *tzedakah*, relatives come first (see *Yoreh Dei'ah* 3, *Hilchos Tzedakah* 251:3). So, too, in doing *kiruv*, relatives come first.

How, then, can you balance the legitimate need to safeguard your children's *Yiddishkeit* and still fulfill your responsibility to care for and about the spiritual growth of your not-yet-*frum* relatives?

I believe that a significant part of the answer lies in the venue. Let me explain.

If you hope to protect your children's *hashkafah* by insuring that they never hear the word "Internet," you will be dismally disappointed. As soon as they are outside of your home, they will hear about many things which are antithetical to Torah. If these things were never discussed or even mentioned in your home, then your children will be ill equipped to deal with them when they are encountered. On the other hand, if you have made your home a proper *beis medrash* where your children can learn how to understand and deal with these issues from a Torah perspective, then you have properly prepared your children for the challenges they will inevitably face in the world outside.

Just as the Internet needs to be *discussed* in any Torah home, so too how to respond to questions raised by not-yet-*frum* relatives also needs to be addressed. You cannot expect that your children will never hear these questions. They most certainly will, whether you like it or not. But you can decide *where* your children will hear them.

Will your children fend off challenges to their *hashkafah* in the "semi-private" venue of your *succah* or in the completely private atmosphere of a bus stop or a street corner? That choice is yours. But I believe they will be far better off if these encounters take place in your home, with your support and under your supervision.

Ask any *kiruv* professional — as you are a *ba'al teshuvah*, undoubtedly you know a few — and they will tell you the undeniable fact that more than the *ba'alei teshuvah* have gained by debating them at their Shabbos table, their children have grown by witnessing and participating in these discussions.

Finally, let me assure you that I have practiced in my own home what I am preaching to you. I have invited not-yet-*frum* guests for Shabbos. And I have encouraged them to pepper me with their questions. On occasion, they even challenged my children.

"If you're not planning to become a rabbi, then why are you still learning in yeshivah?" one of our guests once grilled my son. I then leaned back, *schepping* infinite *nachas* as my son eloquently elaborated on the priceless value of *Torah lishmah*.

4
Young Adults and Beyond

Our 23-Year-Old Son Has Not Developed a Strong Rebbi/Talmid Relationship With Anyone

Something has been bothering me lately and I would like to "pick your brain" about it.

Our son, who happens to be our oldest child, is 23 years old. He is learning in a large, mainstream yeshivah that enjoys a world-class reputation. He has good *chavrusos* and, from what I can tell as his father, seems to be progressing nicely with his learning.

Before he came to this yeshivah, he was learning in Eretz Yisrael for a year and a half at one of the better known yeshivahs in Yerushalayim that caters to Americans. And before that, he put in four years of *mesivta* in town and then three years of *beis medrash* at one of the top not-too-out-of-town yeshivahs.

As you can see, his "resume" is fairly standard and certainly one regarding which my wife and I are extremely proud.

Why, then, you may be wondering, am I writing to you? What concerns me is that in all of our son's "travels" through the yeshivah world, he has not managed to develop a strong rebbi/*talmid* relationship with anyone. Oh, he has whom to go to with his halachic questions. And he even found someone he felt comfortable consulting about one or two *shidduchim*-related questions here and there. But the close, intimate, and ongoing relationship I enjoy with my rebbi is something my son does not experience firsthand.

Yes, I have discussed this with him. And whenever I bring it up he claims that none of his friends or *chavrusos* have that kind of relationship with anyone either.

Do you feel that this is something I should not make such a big deal about? Have times changed and this is no longer necessary today? Or, do you feel that there is something missing in the program if a *bachur* has reached this stage without having developed a strong rebbi/*talmid* relationship with at least one of his rebbe'im?

As you sound like a *ben Torah* yourself, I need not remind you of the *mishnah*, "Asseh l'cha rav; appoint for yourself a rebbi" (*Avos* 1:6). This teaching is repeated later in the same *perek* (*Avos* 1:16). On that second *mishnah*, the Tiferes Yisrael comments, "Appoint for yourself a rebbi . . . to consult with him in order to remove yourself from doubt."

No, I do not believe that a close rebbi/*talmid* relationship is no longer needed today. In fact, it is probably even *more* important today than in past generations. The spiritual *nisyonos* (challenges) our young people face nowadays are at least as formidable as those our ancestors confronted. And a solid rebbi/*talmid* relationship is one of the essential weapons available to protect a *bachur* from the negative influences and pitfalls so prevalent today.

If you have been privileged to develop a closeness with your own rebbi, you know how helpful that has been to you in all areas of your life and in your spiritual development. It is relevant to ask, therefore: Why are many young men going through the yeshivah system today without acquiring this essential Torah asset?

First, we must put all of this in proper perspective. Many *bachurim* do develop close rebbi/*talmid* relationships today. The rebbe'im are certainly open, and, in most cases, eager for it themselves. However, it does require some initiative on the part of the *bachur*.

Some *bachurim* are more shy, by nature. They are not comfortable approaching a rebbi to launch a conversation. They are hesitant to ask personal questions. And they think twice before they pose a *she'eilah* in learning because they are fearful of appearing unlearned.

Other *bachurim*, who are generally relaxed and calm, may experience heightened anxiety whenever they try to think of something to say or ask when one of their rebbe'im walk by or is standing alone. Their mind goes blank for the moment and then they lose the opportunity.

Another reason some *bachurim* never fulfill the *mishnah* quoted above is that the rolling-stone progression of two years at this yeshivah and three years at the next makes it more difficult for many *bachurim* to cultivate a long-lasting connection with any one rebbi.

By the time a *bachur* reaches the age of *shidduchim*, as your son has, it is almost too late to turn back the clock. The advice, support, and guidance he needs to navigate this tortuous path he may seek from his *chaveirim*, with whom he has already established higher levels of comfort and deeper levels of trust.

Finally, on a more positive note, it is entirely possible that some boys feel they do not need a father figure in their life because their relationship with their own father is so satisfactory. Your son, for example, may feel that he can turn to you for guidance and support. He may feel that you understand him so well, care for him so much and advise him so successfully that *you* are his de facto rebbi.

Certainly, there may be other factors that contribute to the phenomenon you described so articulately in your well-written letter. Regardless of the reasons for this predicament, however, the more important question is: What can you, as a father, do to improve the situation and help your son?

You have apparently already set an excellent example for your son by cultivating your own solid relationship with your rebbi. Have you, however, included your son in that relationship? Have you brought your son along with you when you visited or consulted with your rebbi? And, has your son felt included in that special club to which you and your rebbi belong?

A close and dear friend of mine, for example, once invited me to attend the *tefillin leigen* of one of his sons. This friend was a *talmid* of Harav Avraham Pam, *ztz"l*, so he brought his son to Yeshivah Torah Vodaas on that special day. It must be at least 20 years ago, yet I still feel the warmth Harav Pam, *ztz"l*, exuded as he tenderly assisted the *bar mitzvah* boy with putting on his *tefillin* for the first time.

More than the Torah thoughts Harav Pam shared that morning at the modest "*kiddush*" after davening, the affection he demonstrated remains indelibly etched in my memory, and presumably the memories of my friend and his son. And I recall thinking, as I reached for another one of the fresh cinnamon rugalach, that this *bar mitzvah* boy was being initiated not only into the sacred *mitzvah* of wearing *tefillin*. He was also being introduced to the very special rebbi/*talmid* relationship his father enjoyed with one of the *gedolim* of our generation.

Returning to your questions, while times have indeed changed, a strong rebbi/*talmid* relationship is even *more* important now than ever before. For those who are privileged to enjoy one, it provides an anchor and safe harbor that can protect a young man from the myriad dangers lurking within the choppy seas of the modern world. And, therefore, I do believe it is unfortunate if a young man your son's age has "gone through the system" and has not succeeded in developing a strong relationship with any of his rebbe'im or *roshei hayeshivah*.

There are crises, dilemmas, and critical crossroads in life when there will be no adequate substitute for a strong bond with a former rebbi or *rosh hayeshivah*. There will always be *rabbanim* who are available for consultation and support. You cannot compare, however, the value of a recent acquaintance with a long-term relationship forged in youth and spanning a lifetime.

Finally, I must remind you that at 23, your son is certainly not an old man. And he still has many opportunities in life to develop the rebbi/*talmid* relationship that he is missing. Perhaps he will meet a *rosh kollel, rosh chaburah* or *mashgiach* some day with whom he will make a meaningful connection. As long as he has learned from your example how beneficial that relationship can be, there is still hope that someday he will enjoy the bountiful fruits that can grow from a successful rebbi/*talmid* relationship.

Why Is Our Son So Indecisive Regarding Shidduchim?

Our 23-year-old son has entered the challenging world of *shidduchim* and seems to be experiencing some difficulty. My husband and I are at our wits' end and feel totally incapable of helping him. We are desperate for any advice or recommendations you can offer.

Our son is the third of six children. His older two siblings are both happily married. And he is next in line. He began *shidduchim* about five months ago. So far he has met four girls. The first two he was not interested in at all. The third girl he really liked and she wanted to get engaged. As he did not feel ready to finalize a commitment, they mutually agreed to break off with each other. The fourth girl he met only once and decided she was not for him.

Now he is telling us that he thinks he may have made a mistake about breaking it off with girl #3. When we suggest that he go back and meet her again, however, he objects, saying he is still not ready to get engaged to her.

As it stands now, he says he still likes girl #3 a lot and even confesses to thinking about her all the time. On the other hand, he also tells us that there are things about her which he is not sure he can accept and live with.

We have encouraged our son to discuss his dilemma with his rebbe'im which he has done. Whenever he comes home, however, he always tells us that they were not too helpful and he is just as confused and indecisive.

Both my husband and I approved of all four girls he has seen. We do recognize that we cannot make this decision for him and we are frightened that he may be unable to make it for himself.

What could cause such a top *bachur* to be so indecisive and what can we do to help him?

Your son's indecision does sound extreme. Not having met your son, however, I am unable to pinpoint the exact cause of his difficulties. Based on my experience with others, however, I can speculate as to what some of the possibilities might be.

✓ Fear of separation. Some young people become very anxious at the prospect of separating from their parents. These are the same children who fussed over getting on the school bus, were homesick at overnight camp, and hesitated about attending yeshivah or seminary in Eretz Yisrael. For these young people, then, marriage represents the ultimate separation. As the Torah states, "Therefore a man shall abandon his father and mother and cling to his wife" (*Bereishis* 2:24).

✓ Fear of imperfection. Some young people are perfectionistic in the sense that everything has to be just so. All decision-making is complicated for them by this need to fulfill their ideal image of everything. Selecting a tie or a pair of shoes can become an agonizingly elongated process of wading through countless considerations. The slightest flaw becomes magnified and blown way out of proportion, making them unable to live comfortably with any decision they make. Deciding on *shidduchim* then becomes a nightmare because these people believe perfection is possible in *shidduchim*. After all, they say to themselves, look at _____. (S)he found a perfect *shidduch*. So why can't I?

✓ Fear of failure. Some young people suffer from low self-esteem and feelings of inferiority. Their damaged egos make them yearn for popularity, admiration, and respect. Their self-doubts and feelings of inadequacy, however, cause them to be self-critical and expect failure. Since they lack confidence in themselves and their own judgment, they seek unrealistic external reassurance that they are not making a mistake. And because no one can *prove* to them that this or that *shidduch* is the right one for them, they are terrified of making such a long-term commitment to the "wrong" choice in *shidduchim*. And even when they meet someone who is compatible, they are plagued with the nagging doubt that perhaps the next *shidduch* would be even better.

✓ Fear of feelings. Most young people are capable of making major decisions in life, including those related to *shidduchim*, without undo stress and anxiety. This is because they are fully in touch with and aware of their personal feelings. Not only do they know what they like and why, but they also are capable of prioritizing their feelings. As a result, they are able to weigh the pros and cons in order to resolve complex dilemmas.

Some young people, however, never learned or were never encouraged to access their own feelings. Without this critical information, therefore, they are like pilots trying to fly airplanes with their eyes closed. A most terrifying proposition, to be sure.

All of this sounds so irrational, you might argue. Perhaps your son has some very legitimate concerns? How can I be so sure that his reservations are not legitimate?

If your son had a sound reason for not going ahead with *shidduch* #3, he would have shared it with you or with one of his rebbe'im. Then you or the rebbi would have validated his concerns that would have caused him to feel relieved and ready to move on. The fact that he is so stuck now is a clear indication that this is not at all about this particular girl. It is about his irrational fears and excessive anxiety that would probably prevent him from moving forward with any *shidduch* prospect.

I have worked, for example, with similar young men who each told me that they felt there was something unattractive about the girl's nose. As long as the dating was not serious, the shape of the girl's nose did not bother them. As soon as an engagement was discussed, the nose suddenly became much more prominent. Then, when the girl eventually broke off the relationship, the young men "discovered" that the nose was never really a serious issue. Obviously, the girl's nose did not change in size from one date to the next. It became, however, a barometer of the young men's anxiety levels regarding the relationship.

To answer your second question, therefore, the best way to help your son is to show him a copy of this column. If he identifies with any of the fears listed above, encourage him to meet with a therapist who can help him overcome whichever fears are crippling his *shidduchim* decision-making. Once he has resolved the underlying issue holding him back, he will then be free to trust his feelings and judgment which, in turn, will allow him to move forward.

My 26-Year-Old Son
Has No Direction in Life

My son is 26 years old and does not seem to be doing very much with his life. He gave up full-time yeshivah about two years ago, saying that he wanted to go to college. We were not happy about that but felt we could not stop him. He took a couple of courses and decided after one semester that college was not for him. He has had a few part-time jobs but nothing that lasted more than a month or two. Currently, he does some kind of selling over the Internet. I do not know how much he earns from this but he doesn't need too much money as he is still living at home.

My wife and I both feel that our son is wasting his life. And we have told him so. He sleeps late every day. But who could blame him? He really has nothing to get up for.

Most of his friends are already married, pursuing careers in learning, business or professions. They are having children and, I'm sure, giving their parents much *nachas*.

While I would love some *nachas* too, my main concern here is for my son. I feel it is such a shame for him to be wasting his time. I wish I could help him find some direction in life. Can you offer any suggestions?

In his parenting classic, *Z'riah U'binyan B'chinuch* (Feldheim, '95), Harav Shlomo Wolbe, *ztz"l*, distinguished between two mechanisms for development: growth and building. The latter process requires man's direct input at every stage. To erect an edifice, for example, one must lay the foundation and add each floor until the structure is completed.

Growth, on the other hand, dictates that man provide the necessary conditions of water, soil, and sunlight and then remove himself from active involvement while the plants sprout by themselves.

Parenting, according to Harav Wolbe, *ztz"l*, involves a combination of building and growth. If, however, parents attempt to only "build the child, without addressing his natural potential for autonomous growth, parents will turn their child into a robot" (p. 12).

When it comes to motivation, therefore, parents simply cannot expect to insert goals into their children in the same fashion as one builds windows or archways into a house. Parents must fulfill their responsibilities to their children in much the same manner as a farmer cultivates his crops. The soil is prepared. The seeds are sown. The field is irrigated. Then the rest is up to the natural forces directed by Hashem. Too often, parents mistakenly assume they can motivate their children through prodding and cajoling. This may relieve the parents somewhat, by deluding them into feeling that they are "doing something." Nevertheless, this rarely helps. And in many cases it is counterproductive.

From your letter, it sounds as if you may be making this same mistake. I can well understand how frustrating it must be for you and your wife to sit by and watch your son being so unproductive. He is sleeping through part of the day and not making very good use of the rest. You must try, however, to see things from his point of view.

While he may not appear to be clearly focused on any career or life goal, he may nevertheless be actively involved in *searching* for his own goals in life. And that process may take him a bit longer than some of his more goal-oriented friends. In the meantime, you must try to be supportive and, most of all, patient.

In some cases, it is helpful for young people, such as your son, who seem to lack direction in life to meet with a therapist. Talking things over with a trained professional can often assist a young person in identifying areas of interest that could be pursued.

Therapy, however, should not be confused with vocational counseling. The goals of therapy are for the patient to get in touch with his own feelings and preferences as a result of the exploratory process guided by the therapist. Vocational counseling is a more structured process of narrowing career choices.

In suggesting therapy for your son, you must be careful not to present it to him as a mechanism to repair some facet of himself that is damaged. If he sees it that way, he will never accept your suggestion. Rather, therapy should be presented as an opportunity to maximize his potential by speaking with someone who can assist him in clarifying and then achieving his own goals. In addition, the therapist may be able to identify impediments that are subconsciously holding your son back from moving on in life.

I recall, for example, one young man, let's call him Avi, with whom I worked not too long ago, who also seemed to be floating through life as his peers were passing him by. He initially sought my assistance to move on after an unsuccessful *shidduch* relationship had ended. At the point when I met with him, his daily routine (or lack thereof) mirrored that of your son and the many others in our community who struggle with similar issues.

Avi came in one day and clearly needed to vent. He described a brief episode that revealed much about his relationship with his parents.

Avi had come into the kitchen late one Shabbos afternoon to make himself a cup of coffee. He had been trying to lose weight and wanted to avoid any high-caloric refreshments.

"What are you doing?" his mother asked, innocently.

"I'm making myself a coffee," Avi replied, matter-of-factly.

"A coffee? Now? That will keep you up half the night. Then you'll get up late tomorrow and that will ruin your whole day."

"Ma, it is still early enough that it won't prevent me from sleeping tonight."

"But there is so much caffeine in coffee. What do you need that for? Why not drink something else?"

Avi then shared with me what he would have liked to have said to his mother. "Ma, why must you micromanage everything about my life? All I wanted to do was make myself a simple cup of coffee. Why does this have to turn into such a major struggle? At 22, don't you think I'm old enough to decide for myself what beverage to drink on a Shabbos afternoon?"

Avi was having difficulty finding direction in life, in part, because his parents were trying too hard to decide for him. After he began assuming responsibility for making the small decisions in life, however, Avi was eventually able to move on to make larger, more substantive decisions.

Returning to your son, after explaining what you should not do with him, let me give you some instructions about what you should do. Sit back and wait, patiently of course, until he expresses some wish, intention or plan of his own. Then jump at the opportunity to support and encourage his initiative. Be sure, however, that you do not fall into the common pitfall of judging or evaluating his ideas.

More specifically, suppose he announces that he is thinking about becoming a psychotherapist. Instead of scoffing at the notion and verbalizing your skepticism, tell him, "That sounds like a wonderful profession. You could really help a lot of people that way and perform the *mitzvah* of *chesed*."

Certainly, there is a good chance that he may not follow through or even get started. If he has heard your support of his idea, however, that may help to bolster his emerging motivation that will bear more substantial fruit further down the road.

What I am recommending may sound to you as if I am advising you to simply sit by and allow your son to flounder. You may wonder, "But shouldn't he be learning to assume responsibility? Shouldn't he be doing something productive, anything at all, while he is trying to figure out what he wants to do with his life?"

In case that is how you feel, consider this. Many adults do not enjoy their occupation. Nevertheless, they still perform their duties out of a sense of responsibility. If they are working, however, they are still earning a salary. And they have decided that, at least for the time being, it is worth it to them to continue working in order to continue to receive their check.

Suppose these people were told that their salary was now going to be given to someone else. They will now earn nothing. Few, if any, would remain on the job.

Expecting a young person to engage in an activity because it will satisfy his parents but not himself is similar to asking someone to work while his salary is paid to someone else. We are all motivated by self-interest. To expect a young person to act differently is to be totally unrealistic. Parents, therefore, cannot hope to superimpose their goals onto their children and expect that to motivate them. Rather, they must encourage and support their children's ambitions. And they may even have to wait, in some cases, until the first buds begin to sprout before they can offer that encouragement. There is simply no way to speed up or jump-start that natural process called growth.

Our 20-Year-Old Daughter Spends Too Much Money

My wife and I enjoy reading your column each week and we thought perhaps you would also be able to help us with a parenting challenge we are facing.

Our youngest child, a 20-year-old daughter, is now attending a post-seminary academic-degree program and working part-time in a yeshivah office. She is also "on the market," so to speak, as she has entered the *parshah* of *shidduchim*. She is bright, talented, hard working, and quite popular with her friends.

What concerns us, however, is the way she is constantly asking both of us, especially my wife, for money. It is not just "nickels and dimes" for toiletries and cosmetics. It is also for more expensive items such as shoes, clothing, and vacations.

Our daughter works very hard for the pittance she earns at her job. And we feel she should be saving all of that for when she gets married. *Baruch Hashem*, I am able to support my daughter and am happy to do so. What bothers us, however, is the way in which our daughter treats us as if we were an ATM. She always seems to "need" this item to go with that outfit, etc. And now that she is into *shidduchim*, she feels that she always has to look her best, which we fully understand. But there just does not seem to be any restraints on her spending habits.

What makes matters worse is that her pleas for money often set off heated exchanges that end in hurt feelings on both sides. Our daughter complains we are insensitive to her needs and overly critical of her spending. And we feel she is taking too much advantage of our generosity and is not being careful enough with our money. Recently, an all-out shouting match erupted between my wife and daughter ending in tears on both sides, which is what prompted me to write this letter.

If you could offer any suggestions to us we would be most grateful to you.

**The good news** is that you are not alone. Many parents today will be nodding their heads when they read and identify with your dilemma. As *Chazal* have taught, "*Tzar rabbim nechamah*: when suffering is shared by many, it is a comfort" (*Sefer HaChinuch, mitzvah* 331).

While the situation you describe is quite common, it is also most stressful for each of you. Your daughter is frustrated because she feels she is requesting money only for what she considers to be necessities. Instead of the open hand she is expecting, she finds a narrowed eye which she perceives to be overly critical.

Furthermore, your daughter must feel demeaned by the entire process. Her judgment is constantly being scrutinized by you and your wife. She must come to you for every little thing and probably feels like a beggar knocking on doors.

From your end, you and your wife may feel that you are being exploited by your daughter. In your eyes, she is squandering your hard-earned money and behaving like an irresponsible child and not the mature adult you expect her to be. After all, if she is standing on the threshold of married life, you most certainly want her to be managing her finances in a more adult manner than she is doing currently.

The problem here, as I see it, is that you and your wife have contributed to the problem rather than the solution by the arrangement you have instituted in your home. Once the three of you have agreed that you are giving your daughter full support until she marries, she has no choice other than to "nickel and dime" you to the point of frustration on both sides. The current system in your home may allow you total control and supervision of your daughter's spending. It does not, however, provide any opportunity for her to learn and practice the independent decision-making she will need to run her own home.

Chazal have taught that one of a father's basic responsibilities is to enable his child to become independent. As the *Gemara* states, "A father is obligated to his son to . . . teach him a trade and some say even how to swim. Rabbi Yehudah says, 'Whoever does not teach his son a trade, teaches him to steal'" (*Kiddushin* 29a).

What I would recommend, therefore, is that you adjust your financial arrangement with your daughter so that it fosters more autonomy on her part.

For example, instead of doling out money to her on a purchase-by-purchase basis, you should be giving her a fixed allowance. You could start out on a weekly basis and eventually work up to a monthly or even bimonthly basis.

The first step would be for you to sit down with your daughter and draw up a budget of her regular expenditures. How much money does she think she needs per week or per month? And exactly which items will be included in this budget? Will clothing be included? What about transportation, haircuts, toiletries, etc.?

You are, of course, entitled to negotiate this with her. You need not agree to all of her requests. Ideally, this should be seen as a process and not an event. And you should take into account that even regular expenditures vary from month to month.

Once you have agreed upon the weekly or monthly allowance, then make sure she receives this fixed amount in a timely fashion. Then the rest is up to her. If she runs short, she will have to wait until the next payment. "Borrowing" against the next week or month should not be allowed unless it is a serious emergency.

A serious emergency is not a loophole or excuse for your daughter to use whenever she wants to take advantage of a fantastic sale. It is an extraordinary circumstance that could not have been foreseen or prepared for in any way. By definition, an emergency is a rare occurrence. And if your daughter seems to have regular "emergencies," then you have to go back and renegotiate the terms of her allowance so that she understands the fixed nature of this agreement.

This allowance system will provide enormous advantages to all three of you. Your daughter will be encouraged to economize. If she manages to make do with less, she will be rewarded by savings at the end of the week or month which she can keep or spend on more discretionary items. If she does not allocate her money wisely, she will run out of money too soon and will learn the hard way how to keep within her budget.

In addition, you and your wife will be spared the emotionally draining ordeal of heated confrontations with your daughter. Peace and sanity will then be restored to your home.

Finally, this new arrangement for supporting your daughter will enable her to learn the financial-management skills she will need in order to run her own home after marriage, which will come, *b'ezras Hashem, b'sha'ah tovah u'mutzlachas.*

Our 23-Year-Old Son Feels He Is Unable to Deal With Shidduchim Now

We have a 23-year-old son who came back from Eretz Yisrael this past Succos. He had been learning in yeshivah there for two and a half years. Even though all of his friends are into *shidduchim* now and a few are even married already, our son feels that he is unable to deal with *shidduchim* now.

The reason he feels that way is because he has been having constant headaches ever since he returned from Eretz Yisrael. He did have headaches before he came home but not nearly as intense and frequent as they are now. In addition to the headaches, he also suffers periods of dizziness and lightheadedness which interfere with his learning and concentration.

Initially, we were concerned that he might, *chas v'shalom*, have some neurological problem. But all medical causes have been ruled out by the specialists he has consulted. He has had a CAT scan, an MRI, and numerous blood tests, all of which came back negative, *baruch Hashem*.

We have one older, married daughter and three younger sons, none of whom ever went through anything like this. So far, none of the doctors have been able to pinpoint the cause of our son's condition. Over time, it seems to be getting worse, as he has gradually decreased his *hasmadah*, coming home earlier in the evening and often skipping night *seder* altogether.

Although he is certainly an adult, he is still our child. And as his parents we are eager to help him in any way we can. We feel we are at a dead end and don't know where to turn next.

Have you ever come across anything like this? And, if so, what did you learn from that case (or those cases) which could help us to help our son?

We feel very frustrated about all of this and wish there was something we could do. Please respond as quickly as you can because we all feel stuck right now. And we would like to be able to move ahead as soon as possible.

If the medical specialists who examined your son could not diagnose his condition, it would be presumptuous of me to render a diagnosis without even having seen him myself. Having said that, however, I still can answer your first question.

Yes, I have come across similar symptoms on more than one occasion. In each of those cases, the young men were suffering from "somatisized anxiety." I shall explain what that means.

People sometimes experience elevated levels of worry and fear that are not caused by real dangers. That is called anxiety. In more extreme cases, it can even be experienced as dread or panic. Because the nervousness is generated by irrational concerns, elevated anxiety is considered a symptom of emotional disorder.

Anxiety, itself, can take many different forms. It can be manifested as obsessive ruminations, as catastrophic thinking, and as phobic avoidance of everyday situations, to cite a few examples. In addition, anxiety can be expressed as physical symptoms, such as backaches, headaches, nausea, lightheadedness, and dizziness. In these cases, the physical symptoms are real and can be clinically measured. The root causes of these somatic complaints, however, are purely emotional. In other words, it is the worry and fear that causes the physical symptoms and not the other way around.

All anxiety serves a function similar to pain. While it is certainly unwelcome, pain nevertheless serves a vital purpose by alerting us to a problem that requires our immediate attention. When elaborating on the *Chovos HaLevavos'* teaching to be thankful for every human bodily function, Harav Avigdor Miller, *ztz"l*, once cited the unusual case of a woman who was unable to feel pain. As a result, she was unable to feel when her hands or arms came too close to the fire on her stove and only realized it when she smelled her own flesh burning.

The problem requiring attention is not always readily apparent to one suffering from elevated anxiety. In fact, at times, the anxiety serves the paradoxical function of distracting us from that which we are unable or unwilling to confront on a conscious level.

Dr. Jacob Sarno, an orthopedic surgeon, has been a pioneer in popularizing this fact of human nature. He has written numerous best-selling books on the mind/body connection that essentially reiterate the same point. Physical symptoms that have no medical cause are real but are generated by suppressed feelings and emotions which the individual is trying to avoid. Dr. Sarno is not a mental-health professional; therefore his message has been much more accepted and embraced by the general public.

Since the feelings that your son may be suppressing are not conscious, he will probably require the assistance of a trained psychotherapist to help him identify them and work them through. And, quite frankly, I am somewhat surprised that none of the specialists who examined your son recommended that after all medical causes were ruled out. Of course, it is also possible that they did recommend that but your son chose not to share that with you, or that you (or he) pooh-poohed the whole idea.

Considering the timing of the onset of your son's condition, one possible source of his unconscious anxiety might be precisely the issue of *shidduchim*. While all young people are eager to marry, some are also conflicted about it at the same time. Getting married means moving out and away from home. It means separating from one's family of origin and taking on new, and, to some, overwhelming, responsibilities. Some young people are very uncomfortable and even anxious about that.

Furthermore, some young people feel very insecure, suffering from low self-esteem and feelings of inadequacy. While they manage to cope with those feelings by sticking with their friends, the prospect of being scrutinized by a *shidduch*, and his or her family, is too much for them to handle.

It would be embarrassing for a young person to admit — even to him or herself — that he or she was afraid to leave home or nervous about being evaluated. Headaches, dizziness, and other physical symptoms, however, provide a face-saving justification for a young person to postpone entering into *shidduchim*.

None of this, of course, is conscious. And the young people so afflicted feel and believe that they really want to get married as soon as possible. It is only the lightheadedness or nausea that is disabling them. When they are helped to identify the underlying causes of their anxiety that trigger the physical symptoms, however, they are then able to work through their feelings and return to the mainstream of life.

The best thing you can do for your son, therefore, is show him a copy of this column. Some people find relief simply by gaining insight into the mind/body connection. If your son is not so fortunate, you might suggest that he consult with a therapist who can guide him along the path to his recovery. While I cannot predict the outcome for your son, I can tell you that the success rate for this sort of treatment is extremely high and in most cases recovery can be accomplished without resorting to any medication.

While there is no indication from your letter that you are anything but concerned, supportive, and loving parents, I must point out that sometimes the anxiety of the parents exacerbates that of the child. Many young people, for example, approach *shidduchim* with somewhat elevated levels of anxiety for all the reasons mentioned earlier. When that combines, however, with the parents' fears and apprehensions ("Will we be sought after or rejected?" "Will you get married quickly or take a long time like Uncle Ben?" "Will we be embarrassed or have our family reputation enhanced by this process?" etc.), that makes for a very toxic combination. When that happens, the parents worry out loud about any postponement of the process and that only serves to fan the fires of their child's anxiety.

Our 20-Year-Old Son Suffers Tension Headaches

I read your column with great interest. Like the woman who wrote the letter, I too have a 20-year-old son who just came back from Eretz Yisrael and suffers terribly from headaches. I believe they are called "tension headaches."

He has been suffering for about three years. He has had a CT scan which did not show anything, thank G-d. He has also seen a neurologist and has been on and off medication. But nothing has really helped him.

I would like to mention that my eldest son passed away two years ago at the age of 21. I don't know if this is relevant.

If there is anything at all that you think will help, I would be forever indebted to you. Thank you so much.

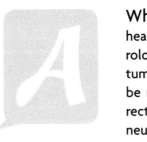

Whenever someone is suffering from headaches for a significant length of time, a neurologist should always be consulted first. Brain tumors and other serious medical conditions must be ruled out right away. Your son took the correct course of action, therefore, by consulting a neurologist and following through on his recommendations for diagnosis and treatment.

If, however, your son has been suffering for three years and, "nothing has really helped him," then it is certainly time to consider another approach.

The fact that your eldest son passed away two years ago may or may not be relevant to your 20-year-old son's headaches. If your eldest son died suddenly from an accident and your 20-year-old's headaches started a year earlier, then there may be no connection between these two issues.

If, however, your eldest son had been battling a terminal illness for at least a year prior to his *petirah*, then that may be extremely relevant to your 20-year-old son's condition.

Chazal have taught us, "Rav said, 'Someone who is *niftar* is only forgotten after a 12-month period [of mourning]'" (*Berachos* 58b). In other words, the normal grieving process typically takes approximately one year. If someone is still plagued by strong emotions of grief, depression, or loneliness beyond 12 months following a loss, that should be considered a case of complicated bereavement that may require some outside help to overcome.

As a result of the dynamics of his relationship with his older brother, his own psychological makeup or both, your 20-year-old son, therefore, may have had an especially difficult time adjusting to his older brother's *petirah*. If he was unable or unwilling to discuss his feelings openly with other members of the family and work them through, he may have tried to suppress his feelings in order to cope with them and "move on."

Whenever someone tries to suppress intense emotions, however, they do not simply go away. Just because one is not consciously thinking about something does not mean that it is fully resolved and no longer a source of stress. On the contrary, suppressed emotions tend to surface in the form of physical symptoms such as backaches, dizziness, lightheadedness, nausea, and even tension headaches.

Once underlying medical conditions have been ruled out by diagnostic tests and consultation with a physician, as in your son's case, then the next step would be to meet with a psychotherapist who has had experience treating similar cases of somatized anxiety.

Such treatment is usually successful but does not relieve the symptoms right away. It often takes many months of therapy before the source of the suppressed feelings can be properly identified and worked through.

If your son is planning to remain here, therefore, I would encourage you to get him started with this therapy as soon as possible. If, however, he is planning to return to Eretz Yisrael soon, he would be better off not starting the therapy now. Instead, he should wait until he gets back to

Eretz Yisrael in order to see a therapist there.

To get started with a therapist in the United States and then continue with another therapist in Eretz Yisrael is definitely not recommended. If your son meets a therapist here, he will have either a positive or negative experience. If he likes the therapist here, he will consequently compare the Israeli therapist unfavorably. This will interfere with a successful outcome. If he does not feel comfortable with the therapist here, he will be reluctant to try therapy again in Eretz Yisrael.

If you need a referral to a fully trained therapist anywhere in Eretz Yisrael, an excellent resource is the international Orthodox mental-health referral-agency Relief. Their phone number in Yerushalayim is 011-972-2-580-8008.

Tension Headaches — Part II

Reading the problem described by the mother whose son had been suffering from headaches for three years, I smelled the all-too-familiar symptoms of TMS, the revolutionary approach to healing chronic back pain, headaches, and fatigue discovered by Dr. John E. Sarno. I suffered for years from a similar issue and *b"H* was helped through this approach . . .

Y.K.
Yerushalayim

You recently wrote about repressed emotions manifesting themselves in chronic headaches. Here in England, my wife and I run the TMS center using the method of Dr. John Sarno of New York . . . Many people have been able to regain their lives, *bs"D*, after only a few sessions. I can be contacted at 07876-343-715.

Danny Rubin
Manchester

Your recent article about tension headaches sounds comparable to the headaches my son has endured for many years which restrict all of his activities severely. You advocate psychotherapy but you don't specify which type. Would any type help?

In your opinion, could our son be helped by a non-Jewish psychotherapist? In our situation, to see a *frum*, Jewish practitioner would involve a full day's journey.

Lastly, after one or two meetings, could sessions be successfully conducted over the telephone?

Name Withheld
England

Of all the topics I have addressed, none has elicited such an enormous response as the subject of tension headaches. The three letters above represent but a sample of the mail I have received regarding this issue. Apparently, many people in our community suffer from physical ailments caused by repressed emotions.

The Sarno method, referred to in the first two letters, is very effective and has helped thousands of people overcome their debilitating conditions. It does not, however, work for everyone. And I have firsthand knowledge that Dr. Sarno, himself, has referred some of his own more difficult cases for psychotherapy.

In response to the third letter, no, not every type of psychotherapy would be recommended for someone suffering from tension headaches. An expressive or psychodynamic psychotherapy would be best suited for treating such cases. While CBT, or cognitive/behavioral therapy, may provide some symptomatic relief, a psychodynamically oriented approach zeroes in on the root of the problem and is therefore more effective.

One young man I treated, for example, suffered from such debilitating spells of weakness and lightheadedness that he spent more and more time at home, curtailing his hours at yeshivah. Eventually, he was able to connect his symptoms to his repressed feelings toward one particular member of his family who had been and still was overly critical and hurtful.

As the therapy proceeded, this young man learned to confront his feelings rather than evade them. And this, in turn, enabled him to resume more normal functioning, including more regular attendance at yeshivah.

As far as telephone-therapy sessions are concerned, there is a wide range of opinions on this question. Some mental-health professionals believe that treatment can be successfully conducted over the phone. I am not one of them. While I have conducted sessions over the phone in my own practice, that was only under emergency circumstances, such as during a heavy snowstorm, and only for a single session. To conduct any *ongoing* therapy over the telephone significantly diminishes the effectiveness and, consequently the success of, that treatment.

Since you live in England, however, before your son undergoes psychotherapy, you might want to try the Sarno approach. It is less costly than psychotherapy and requires a much smaller investment of time. And as with most problems in life, it makes sense to attempt the simpler solutions before the more arduous ones. So you might even want to look into the services described in the letter above yours.

In case you have already attempted the Sarno method and it did not relieve your son of his headaches, then psychotherapy should definitely be considered for him. As you live a day's journey from the nearest *frum* therapist, you are asking me my opinion of his seeing a non-Jewish one.

The question of seeking help from a non-Jewish therapist is a halachic issue on which you should seek guidance from a *poseik* who is well versed and familiar with mental-health matters. All I feel it is appropriate for me to say is that Hagaon Harav Moshe Feinstein, *ztz"l*, wrote a *teshuvah* on this very subject 50 years ago (*Igros Moshe, Yoreh Deah* II, *Siman* 57).

In that *teshuvah*, Rav Moshe wrote that one should not seek treatment from psychologists or psychiatrists who are atheists. Since medicines are not used, he explained, and the therapy is conducted primarily through talking, the therapist could advise the patient in ways which are antithetical to Torah, the fundamentals of *Yiddishkeit*, or the principles of *tznius* and modesty. One must be concerned, therefore, that the therapist may speak words of apostasy or *nivul peh*, foul language.

Rav Moshe concluded his *teshuvah*, however, with the following qualification. "If the psychologists or psychiatrists are experts and they promise the parents [of their patients] that they will not say anything contrary to the beliefs or *mitzvos* of the Torah, perhaps one could rely on [the principle that] since they are experts they will not lie. Therefore, one should seek out a Torah-observant psychiatrist. If none [is available], make up with [the non*frum* therapist] that he will commit himself not to speak with the patient about any matters of religious belief or Torah."

Our 24-Year-Old Son
Spends Much of His Day in His Room

Our 24-year-old son has been gradually deteriorating over the last couple of years. We are very concerned and are at a loss as to how to help him.

He is the oldest of five children. The other four are successfully pursuing their studies in mainstream yeshivahs and Bais Yaakovs. They each have many friends and outside interests. And they each are happy and well adjusted.

Our oldest was also doing well at yeshivah until his second year of *bais medrash*. It was then that he decided to leave yeshivah to attend college, which he did for almost two years. Since he dropped out of college he has not worked for more than a few weeks at any full- or part-time job. Now he spends much of his day in his room and has little contact with friends. He does not attend *minyan* and lately his *kiyum hamitzvos* has slackened off dramatically. He also stays up quite late at night and sleeps for most of the day.

We did try to encourage him to see a therapist about six months ago. He went for two or three sessions and then dropped out of that, too. He complained it was not helping and was a waste of time and money, even though we were paying for it.

Whenever we manage to engage him in conversation, which is quite rare these days, he is extremely negative. He rejects any suggestions we make and finds fault with any plan we offer. As time goes on, he seems to be getting worse and we simply do not know what more we can do to help him.

We enjoy reading your column each week and thought perhaps you might be able to guide us.

Your son is displaying all of the classical symptoms of clinical depression. He has become socially withdrawn. His daily routine and sleeping pattern are impaired. He has lost interest in activities that used to be pleasurable to him. And he is feeling down, demoralized, and hopeless.

The fact that he is unproductive during the day is only exacerbating his condition. As *Chazal* have said, "Idleness leads to mental illness" (*Kesubos* 59b).

Exactly what precipitated your son's decline remains a mystery to me and, perhaps, to you as well. While that can and should be looked into, the more immediate concern is what you can do now to reverse your son's deterioration.

First, you must make a conscious decision to suspend any and all criticism of your son's behavior. Clearly, there is much to criticize him for — that he is not doing what he should, as well as that which he is doing that he should not — but any criticism from you at this point would be totally counterproductive. To someone as depressed as your son, even the slightest form of criticism feels like being beaten when you are already down.

In a similar vein, therefore, it is also necessary for you to refrain from making suggestions because someone who is depressed tends to take advice as a more subtle form of criticism. Recommendations such as, "Why don't you try. . .?" or, "How about calling. . .?" may be very well intentioned. Nevertheless, to a depressed person, they are viewed as a put-down.

For example, your son could hear your advice as blame, as if you were telling him, "The only reason you are depressed is because you are not doing what you are supposed to do. It is all your own fault." He could also hear your advice as an insult, as if you were telling him, "You have no good ideas of your own. Only we know what is best and you don't."

If your son refuses therapy and you cannot give him any advice, are you then supposed to sit by and watch him deteriorate further? Absolutely not! What you must do now is to get him to meet with a psychiatrist who can prescribe the medication he needs.

Now, you may ask, if you have been unsuccessful in getting him to return to therapy, how on earth can you hope to get him to consult with a psychiatrist?! The answer is that you must sit down with your son and make three critical points in your discussion with him.

First, you must tell him that he is depressed. No, you are not a mental-health professional. And, yes, only qualified mental-health professionals are trained to diagnose mental disorders. Nevertheless, you can and should share with him your observation that he certainly seems to you to be depressed. "Anyone who is acting as you are is most likely suffering from depression."

Even people who are severely depressed sometimes do not recognize the symptoms and may deny they are suffering from depression. Labeling their disorder is not meant to stigmatize them or to put them down. On the contrary, it is helpful to them because it gives them an explanation for what they are feeling that does not permit them to blame themselves. "It would be hard for anyone to be productive if they felt as depressed as you do."

The second point you must make is that depression can interfere with a person's ability to engage with and benefit from therapy. He need not see his failed attempt at therapy six months ago, therefore, as an indication of some inadequacy on his part or even on the part of the therapist. "You were probably feeling depressed then, too, and that's why you felt discouraged about the therapy."

In study after study of depression, the research findings come to the same conclusion. The maximum benefit in the shortest time is achieved when therapy is combined with antidepressant medication. Therapy alone can and does help some people, just as medication alone can improve some people's mood. The *combination* of therapy and medication, however, is much more effective and helps almost all who suffer from depression.

The third point you need to make, therefore, is that there is a biological component to depression. As a result, only medication can correct this chemical imbalance which is making life so difficult for him right now. "And since medication can make you feel so much better, it would be a shame for you not to be taking it."

You should then offer to find a psychiatrist with whom your son can meet for a consultation. If the psychiatrist determines that your son does, indeed, need medication, he will write a prescription for him at the first appointment. And once he has begun taking the medication, it may not be long until he is willing to make another attempt at therapy, either with the therapist he met with previously or another one recommended by the psychiatrist.

Since your son has been so negative and has rejected all of your suggestions thus far, you might be skeptical about this plan. I know of many young people, however, who were in circumstances similar to your son's who surprised their parents and did agree to see a psychiatrist. And these same young people ultimately succeeded in overcoming their depression and returned to normal functioning.

In fact, young people who were successfully treated for depression can and do move on to *shidduchim,* marriage and normal family life. How to deal with the sensitive subject of your son's treatment regarding the *shidduch* process is a question which you must discuss with your personal *poseik.* Only he can offer you practical guidelines in this area that are halachically sound while safeguarding your son's best interests.

Our 25-Year-Old, Married Son Has Recently Cut Back on His Contact With Us

Our 25-year-old son has been married for two years and now has a baby of his own. He learns full-time in kollel and lives about a half-hour from us by car. He is a brilliant *ben Torah* and we are extremely proud of his accomplishments. He is the youngest of six children. All the rest are, *b"H*, married with children.

While we enjoy a good relationship with the rest of our children, who all call and visit us regularly, our youngest child has recently cut back dramatically on his calls and visits. He used to keep in touch with us as much as his brothers and sisters and was a perfect child when he was growing up. Lately, however, he has been argumentative, critical, and quite emotionally distant.

My wife and I are so distressed by this alienation we are getting from our youngest child that we even went to speak with one of his rebbe'im about it. The rebbi was most sympathetic and offered to speak with our son. This helped for a week or two. Unfortunately, the improvement did not last.

We would like to know what else we can do to reconcile our relationship with our son before we lose him completely.

Unfortunately, there are many parents who are alienated from adult married children for 10, 20, and even 30 years, causing untold heartache and grief on both sides. In most cases, had those parents reached out for help and guidance earlier, as you are doing now, they could have succeeded in reconciling their differences and resuming the warm, loving relationships they once had with their children.

In your letter, you give no specifics regarding the reduction of contact. How often, for example, did he visit before? How often is he visiting now? How often did he call in the past? How often does he call now? In addition, you gave no indication of what you suspect may have triggered this recent shift in your relationship with your son. In case you have not yet asked him for an explanation, that would be a good place to start.

Is he aware that he has been in contact with you less now than he used to? Is it deliberate or a result of recent stresses at home? If it is deliberate, is there anything which you and/or your wife are doing that is causing him to want to avoid you? Was anything said or done to his wife which hurt or offended her? Needless to say, if your son points to anything in particular, you would need to take that issue quite seriously if you ever hope to rebuild your relationship with him.

Presumably, however, you have already asked those questions and did not receive any useful information. If so, you may be left wondering what on earth could cause an otherwise intelligent person to behave so irrationally.

You also made no reference to your son's relationships with his five siblings. How does he and your daughter-in-law get along with them? Is he in contact with them? And, have there been any recent changes in his relationships with them that parallel the issues described in your letter? In case you do not know, you can and most certainly should ask them.

If you learn that your son has recently cut off from all of his siblings, then he may be reacting to something going on in his private life of which you are unaware. In such a case, all you can do is inquire and try to gently find out, without prying, as much as you can.

On the other hand, if you discover that your son's relationships with his siblings have not changed recently and he is only cutting back on his contact with you and your wife, then we must look at your relationship with him for an explanation of his behavior.

Allow me to speculate, therefore, based on the limited information you provided in your letter. You described your son as having been a "perfect child when he was growing up." Perhaps you mean that he was never disobedient or disrespectful, always did what he was told, and never got into any sort of trouble at home or in yeshivah. If so, that is not the profile of a well-adjusted, happy child.

If a painting or an *esrog* has no flaw or blemish, it may be described as perfect. In reality, however, it is more likely to be a forgery or a *murkav*.

But even if you can find a truly flawless work of art or citron, human beings rarely achieve perfection. In fact, the Torah specifically records the perceived shortcomings of our great forefathers and leaders.

Some children, however, do set this unrealistic standard of perfection for themselves, squelching the slightest stirrings of dissent, discomfort or disagreement. As a result, their behavior may appear "perfect" to the adults around them. In reality, however, they may be suppressing their natural feelings to such an unhealthy extent that serious psychological or emotional problems may emerge later.

I recall one such "perfect" child, let's call him Aron, who was described as "bright" by his parents and "perfectly behaved" but, nevertheless, was performing well below his abilities in yeshivah. A full battery of psychological tests were administered, revealing significant mental disturbance caused by Aron's desperate attempt to live up to what he saw as his parents' unrealistic expectations of him.

Together with his parents, I launched a campaign to help Aron set more realistic goals for himself. "You'll know that our work has succeeded," I told Aron's parents almost 25 years ago, "when, some day, you will get a phone call from Aron's yeshivah that he was thrown out of class for misbehavior." And I still recall the choked, emotional voice of his mother when she called me a year later to thank me and share the "*nachas*" that she had just received the phone call from Aron's principal that I had predicted.

Coming back to your dilemma with your son, it is entirely possible that the surge of independence brought on by marriage and parenthood has uncovered longstanding oppositional feelings toward you and/or your wife. In the past, he may have been too timid, compliant or frightened to express them. Even now, he may not be expressing those feelings openly and directly. Instead, he may only be acting them out through his passive aggressive withdrawal from you.

To put it in more simple terms, your son may be demonstrating through his behavior that he is upset with something about you and/ or your wife. Because of his history of having been a "perfect child," it may be difficult for him to confront you directly by telling you what is bothering him.

If you cannot coax him to explain his feelings to you directly, you may need to go to a mental-health professional who can work with all three of you to facilitate your communication with one another. In the protected atmosphere of a therapist's office, your son may be able to open up and let you know what may be bothering him. Only then will you be able to make the changes necessary to reconcile your relationship with him. Considering what you have to gain by going and what you have to lose by not going, it should be well worth the investment.

I wish you all much *hatzlachah* in overcoming this challenge.

Do We Have to Provide Monetary Assistance Equally to All Our Children?

My wife and I are, *baruch Hashem*, grandparents many times over. Quite frankly, we feel somewhat awkward writing to you with a parenting issue. Nevertheless, we would appreciate whatever insights you could offer.

Our three children are all married and each have children of their own. Our son is a successful businessman. Our older daughter is married to a prominent C.P.A. who also learns part-time in kollel every morning. And our younger daughter is married to a full-time kollel *yungerman*.

Our older two children live in their own homes which they purchased without any financial assistance from us. *Baruch Hashem*, they were each able to afford the full down payments on their own when they purchased their homes.

Our younger daughter and son-in-law live in a tiny, overcrowded three-bedroom apartment together with their six children. They really need to move into a larger apartment but have been putting it off because they cannot afford the added expense.

We feel sorry for them and have offered to help them buy a house. That way they will have more living space and not be as cramped as they are now. In addition, their monthly payments will go toward the mortgage, building future equity, instead of for rent.

The problem now, however, is that our two older children are very resentful. They have not spoken to us openly about this but it has gotten back to us from other relatives that they feel we are showing favoritism toward our younger daughter and son-in-law. Our older children waited until they each could afford to purchase homes on their own, without any financial assistance from us. Our younger daughter, they feel, should do the same.

On the other hand, we feel that our son and older son-in-law are both working. So they each had the opportunity to save up for the down payments on their homes. Our younger son-in-law is still learning full-time. If we do not help him and our younger daughter, they may never be able to have their own home.

The tension that exists now at family gatherings is palpable. We were always a close-knit family before this issue came up. Do you have any advice as to how we can get things back to the way it used to be?

Just because you are grandparents does not mean that you have outgrown your roles as parents. Until "120," you retain that status along with all of the confusion, frustrations, questions, and, of course, *nachas* that are included.

When it comes to *mitzvos*, we use the father/son relationship as the basis for the term *bar mitzvah*. When it comes to *aveiros*, however, we use the husband/wife relationship as the basis for the term *ba'al aveirah*. Why the inconsistency?

I was privileged, many years ago, to hear Harav Pinchas Breuer, *shlita*, answer this question. He explained that the husband/wife relationship is meant to last forever. Under compelling circumstances, however, those ties can be broken. Similarly, a sinner is bound to *aveiros* with a connection that we hope will also be severed.

Parents and children, on the other hand, have a connection that can never be broken. And we call a 13-year-old boy a *bar mitzvah* to remind him that his responsibility to observe *mitzvos* can also never be shirked. So you need not feel awkward at any age to seek guidance in your permanent roles as parents.

Now, to your question.

All important messages should be delivered directly. While this is true in all areas of life, it is even more critical in family relationships. Resolving conflicts between family members is complicated enough without adding the layers of misunderstanding that inevitably result from communicating through intermediaries.

The first thing you need to do, therefore, is cut out the "other relatives" and speak directly to your children about this issue. It was not clear from your letter whether or not your children know that these other relatives spoke to you about their feelings. In order to avoid the possibilities for *rechilus*, therefore, you should not mention the relatives' names.

You can begin the conversation by asking your older children if they sense any tension at family gatherings. If they acknowledge the absence of closeness now, ask them what they see as the cause. If they do not bring up the money issue then you should be probing if they have any feelings about your helping your younger daughter. (You should be speaking to them separately about this and not as a group. That way they will be less likely to gang up on you.) If they pretend that it does not bother them, mention the tension you have experienced recently and ask what that is all about.

If they acknowledge hurt feelings, do not become defensive. It is an important part of the resolution process for them to air their sentiments with you. Ask them exactly what bothers them and what they would want or expect from you. Trying to understand their feelings does not mean you are committing yourselves to carry out their bidding. It simply means that their feelings are important to you and you take them seriously.

If your children ask you for more details, such as exactly how much money you are giving to your younger daughter, you should gently decline to share that information. It is simply not appropriate for them to know. Healthy parent/adult-child relationships are maintained when parents do not share such detailed information about one child with another.

If your older children express the resentment that your other relatives conveyed to you, you should explain to them some basic truths about family life which they apparently have not yet learned. Families are not democracies. They are not governed by majority rule. Rather, they operate more on the basis of what used to be called the communist manifesto: "each according to his abilities and each according to his need."

Children are not dealt with in cookie-cutter similarity. If one child has fever, all children are not brought to the doctor's office. Fairness does not require that all children receive the same-size clothing. Fairness means that parents will evaluate each child's individual needs with the same concern and devotion.

If you had been able to help your older children financially, it probably would have been a good idea to have offered to help them, even nominally, when they purchased their homes. And you can acknowledge that not having done so was probably a mistake. Nevertheless, your younger daughter's financial situation is much different from theirs. And your initiating an offer to help her was done with that difference in mind.

Timing is also a factor that may be playing a role here. Years ago when your older children were buying their homes you may not have had as much disposable income as you do now. Younger children always have older parents with all of the advantages and disadvantages that come along with that.

The bottom line in all of this, which you need to emphasize over and over, is that your love for one child should not be measured by how much help you give to another child.

It is important to emphasize to your older children that how you spend your money is not a matter under their jurisdiction. You earned it, after all. And you get to dispense it as you see fit. Just as they would not appreciate your telling them what to do with their money, let them know that you do not appreciate their telling you what to do with yours.

Some children – and I am not suggesting that your children fall into this category – see their parents' wealth as their future *yerushah* (inheritance). When viewed in that light, any money given to one child means less to be divided up "after 120." Such children need to understand that "until 120" their parents' money belongs *only* to their parents. And their parents have every right to use it or give it away as they see fit.

Finally, it is healthier all around if parents do not discuss details of their parenting of one child with any other child. As children get older and become parents themselves, they sometimes feel entitled to weigh in on parenting decisions their parents make regarding younger siblings. While children are entitled to their feelings and opinions, they are not entitled to pass judgment on their parents' handling of situations involving their siblings. As my brother-in-law Ezra Beyman often says, "Nowadays children feel that it is getting harder and harder to bring up parents."

My Childless Friend Seems Uncomfortable Whenever I Mention My Children

We have, *baruch Hashem*, a 2-year-old son and a daughter who is almost 6 months old. While they are both quite a handful, I am grateful every day for the privilege of parenthood Hashem has granted to us. In fact, I am not writing to you about them, per se, and I was even hesitant to contact you since my question is not directly related to parenting. But my husband encouraged me to write (he values your opinion as much as I do). And we are both hoping you will address my question in your column.

I have a close friend from high school who moved into the same building complex where I live. We married a few months apart and were delighted to renew our friendship as newlyweds. We had attended different seminaries after high school and both worked for a year before marriage.

Unfortunately, my friend is still childless. And we are both married a little over three years.

Until my baby was born, I did not notice any indication that my friend felt uncomfortable whenever I mentioned or dealt with my son. Now that I have a second child, however, it seems that my friend is somewhat ill at ease whenever I tend to or mention my children.

My husband feels that I should not make any attempt to "shield" my friend from the fact that we have two children. As we live in a kollel complex where there are literally wall-to-wall children, he feels it is unavoidable for her to be confronted by other people's children. He feels, therefore, that it would be unrealistic for me to hope to lessen her ordeal by monitoring my speech whenever I speak with her.

I, on the other hand, wonder if, perhaps, I should try to be more sympathetic to her *nisayon*. I can imagine that she must be suffering greatly and I would not want to do anything which might increase her pain even slightly.

What would you recommend?

No, your question does not deal with parenting, although it does have a lot to do with parenthood. My main motivation in selecting your letter for this week's column is because it gives me the opportunity to applaud you for your exemplary *middos* and sensitivity. Others in your situation would shake their heads, mutter, "such a *rachmanus!*" and then turn their attention back to their own lives. The fact that you took the time to write about this testifies that you possess the quintessential Jewish traits of *"rachmanim v'gomlei chassadim."*

More specifically, your letter demonstrates the highest standards of fulfilling the *middah* of being *"nosei b'ol im chaveiro,* helping to carry your friend's burden" (*Pirkei Avos* 6:6). On this *mishnah*, the *Medrash Shmuel* writes, "The intent [of this *middah* is that] when one sees his friend in pain, he suffers along with him."

The excruciating pain of infertility is well beyond the comprehension of most people who themselves have been blessed with children. Some of these people may even think to themselves, *We cannot really do anything to lessen the pain of their childlessness. So we might as well just go about our lives, "business as usual."*

Personally, I do not believe that satisfies the criteria of the *Medrash Shmuel* for fulfilling the *middah* of being *nosei b'ol im chaveiro.* Your concern and sensitivity, however, does suggest that you are feeling, or at least, attempting to feel, your friend's distress and heartache.

If a doctor could only prolong someone's life for six months, should he say to his patient, "Since you are going to die soon anyway, I might as well not treat you"? If a doctor could only reduce someone's physical pain, should he say to his patient, "Since you are still going to suffer anyway, I might as well not give you any pain-relieving medication"?

No, you cannot *completely* relieve your friend's enormous pain caused by her infertility. But that most certainly should not deter you from doing whatever you can to soften the blow and ease her burden.

Needless to say, you can and must daven for her and her husband to be blessed with children soon. But do not make the mistake of encouraging her to daven with more *kavannah*. Peninah used that strategy with Chanah, the mother of Shmuel *HaNavi*. And in spite of her good intentions (see Rashi on *Shmuel I* 1:6), it had disastrous results for Peninah (see Rashi on *Shmuel I* 2:5).

It is important to bear in mind that many childless couples are hurt more when parents walk on eggshells in their presence. They sense the efforts made to eliminate children from the conversation and consequently feel worse if their friends bend over backward to avoid any references to their kids. These couples very much want their friends to act normally in their presence so as not to highlight their problem and make them feel pitied.

From your letter, however, it is apparent that your friend does not fit into that category. As you wrote, she "is somewhat ill at ease whenever [you] tend to or mention [your] children." In her particular case, therefore, adopting your husband's approach may not be what is best for her.

Since I do not know your friend, I certainly cannot speak for her. What I can tell you, however, is that some *ba'alei nisayon* feel that their *nisayon* is like the elephant in the room that everyone sees but no one mentions. These people often feel relieved and even appreciated when others acknowledge their plight.

Sometimes, the greatest *chizuk* you can offer to *ba'alei nisayon* is to let them know that you care, that you feel for them, that you feel *with* them, and that you daven for them. And in the final analysis, I believe that is what the *Medrash Shmuel* really meant by "suffering along with him."

In order to illustrate how one can fulfill the *middah* of being *nosei b'ol im chaveiro* with someone who has not yet been blessed with children and still not make him or her feel pitied, let me share with you the following true story I heard from the *ba'al middos* himself.

A kollel couple had been childless for almost four years before they were blessed with a baby girl. Someone in the kollel apartment building in which they lived was so happy for his neighbor that he hung a "Mazel Tov it's a girl!" sign on the front door of the new parents' apartment.

The next day, the sign had been removed. Another neighbor met the new father in the hall and asked him, "Why did you take the 'Mazel Tov' sign down? Are you disappointed that it was not a boy?"

"Are you kidding?" asked the new father, rhetorically. "My wife and I are *thrilled* beyond words with the new baby. We are so grateful to Hashem that we do not know how to express ourselves adequately."

"Then why did you take down the 'Mazel Tov' sign? Was there something about the sign you did not like?" his neighbor persisted.

"Don't you realize that there is another couple living in our building who do not yet have children?" the new father asked, again rhetorically. "Until now, it was only us and them. Now they are the *only* childless couple in the entire building. I am very happy with the sign. And I wish I knew who put it up so I could thank him. But I removed it and placed it on the *inside* of my front door because that couple has to pass my apartment on the way to theirs. And I did not want them to see that sign and feel even one more prick of pain whenever they would enter or leave the building."

"But there are children, carriages, and toys all over the halls and yard 24/7," the neighbor objected. "It is impossible to walk in or out of this building and not be reminded of children. How does your taking down the 'Mazel Tov' sign help them?"

"How long did you have to wait for children after you were married?" the new father asked.

"We did not have to wait. We had children right away."

"Then that explains it. You see, we did not have children for almost four years. And *we* can understand that every reminder adds another stab. So if we could eliminate just one of those stabs, then we jumped at the chance."

Ashrei yeladito, happy are the parents who bore such an outstanding *ba'al middos*!

How Can I Prevent My 21-Year-Old Son from Smoking?

My son will be 21 years old next month. And we are planning to send him to learn in Eretz Yisrael after Succos, iy"H. He is our oldest boy so this will be our first experience with a yeshivah in Eretz Yisrael.

We are all very much looking forward to this next, exciting step in his growth in learning. He has done well in *mesivta* and *beis medrash* so we are eagerly anticipating this new opportunity. He will be attending a well-respected, world-renowned citadel of Torah together with some of his closest *chaveirim*.

Baruch Hashem, the security situation in Eretz Yisrael now is relatively calm, and I am not especially worried for his physical safety. He has always been a responsible young man. And he has earned our trust. Therefore, I am not concerned that he will risk traveling in areas that might be unsafe, *chas v'shalom*.

What troubles me as a parent, however, as we continue to talk and plan for this major event, is that I do not want my son to come home having "learned" to smoke. Unfortunately, I know of too many fine young men from excellent homes who go to learn in Eretz Yisrael for a year and return hooked on cigarettes.

Smoking is a nasty, expensive habit. We are all well aware of the serious health risks involved. And, nowadays, smoking is even a liability when it comes to *shidduchim*. The better girls — including my own daughters — would never think of meeting a *bachur* who smokes. In spite of all that, however, we still see many *bachurim* from our neighborhood return from Eretz Yisrael with a newly acquired addiction to smoking.

Is there anything I can do now, before my son leaves, which can protect him from this scourge?

Your son is fortunate to have you as his parent. If more parents asked this question, we would see much less smoking in our community.

Baruch Hashem, smoking is definitely on the decline in America. The antismoking movement in this country has even succeeded in penetrating our own community. And this is one of the few examples of the larger society having a positive impact on the Torah world. Unfortunately, however, Eretz Yisrael needs to catch up with us in this regard. So your concern is definitely justified.

Before suggesting what steps you can take to inoculate your son against smoking, let me first outline the misguided and ineffective strategies that parents tend to use most often.

✓ Lecturing on the evils of smoking. Lectures may be filled with Torah sources and scientific facts. Quoting "*V'nishmartem m'od l'nafshoseichem*" (*Devarim* 4:15) may strengthen your argument, but it will do little to impact the behavior of a young adult who claims, "I know I'll stop *before* I become hooked. So none of that applies to me."

✓ Monitoring friends. Of course you should get to know who your son's friends are. That is one of the ways in which parents demonstrate interest in the lives of their children. But you cannot expect to prevent your son from smoking by scrutinizing all of his social contacts. At 21, your son must choose his own friends.

✓ Constant interrogation. You could ask your son every week whether or not he smoked that week. But all that will accomplish is to teach him to be dishonest. Almost every boy experiments at some point by "taking a puff." If they feel the need to lie to their parents about that, it will make it easier for them to lie if and when they smoke the next time.

So what can parents do to help shield their children from becoming habitual smokers?

✓ If you are a smoker, quit now. Many parents who smoke feel they are in the best position to discourage their children from following in their footsteps. "My children see how much I suffer," they say. "That should be the greatest deterrent." Unfortunately, however, children are more likely to follow parental examples than parental warnings.

As we say in *kri'as Sh'ma*, *"V'lo sasuru acharei l'vavchem v'acharei eineichem"* (*Bamidbar* 15:39). And Rashi comments on that *pasuk* that what we see is what entices us to sin.

✓ Talk about smoking as often as possible. *Lecturing* is condescending. It implies you are the authority above and your child is the inferior below. Lectures only motivate children to try to prove their parents wrong.

Discussions, on the other hand, are more respectful and egalitarian. They are thoughtful exchanges of ideas that rarely provoke rebellion.

A helpful discussion of smoking would begin with questions designed to elicit your child's thoughts and feelings. Your own ideas and opinions should only be included, gently, at the end, almost as an afterthought. Your feelings, of course, are extremely important and informed by years of solid life experience. To a 19-year-old, however, the judgments of parents are old fashioned, at best, or provocations, at worst. It is far more effective, therefore, to plant seeds to germinate in your son's mind by asking questions.

Some good gambits are: "Do any of your friends smoke?" "What do you think about those guys your age who smoke?" "Do you know anyone who is trying to quit smoking?" "Why do they want to stop and why do you think they are having such a hard time?" "How come those individuals began smoking in the first place and what assumptions do you suppose they were making at that point?"

✓ Maintain a warm, loving relationship with your child. Smoking is one of the most convenient and passive methods of rebellion against parents. If children feel loved and cared for, if they feel respected and appreciated, if their feelings are validated, and if they feel that the limits set for them are fair and reasonable, then they will have no motivation to rebel against parental authority by smoking.

✓ Finally, as with all aspirations we have for our children, we must never underestimate the importance of *tefillah*. And *tefillah* with tears has proven to be the most effective weapons parents can use to protect their children from any danger.

If you implement the strategies outlined above, therefore, I believe you can be hopeful that when your son comes home from learning in Eretz Yisrael, he will not be carrying a pack of cigarettes in his pocket.

"A Final Word"

After all is said and done, after all the shoes are tied and the runny noses wiped, no one can deny that there are few enterprises in life as significant, noble and gratifying as the priceless privilege of raising children. Anyone who doubts this fact needs only to look at the enormous mountains that childless couples eagerly move in order to fulfill their dream of parenthood. When we are engaged in parenting, we literally reach into eternity, as we mold the generation which will shape all future generations. We become the link in the unbroken chain connecting all unborn Jewish children to the *Avos* and *Ma'amad Har Sinai*. And we leave our indelible imprint on the still unwritten pages of the history of the future of our people.

In order to succeed in the lofty mission of Jewish parenting, we must utilize as many tools as we can find in the words of *Chazal*, in public lectures and *shiurim* on *chinuch banim*, in private consultations with *Rabbonim* and senior *mechanchim*, and in parenting books, such as the one you are holding in your hands right now. These tools alone, however, may not guarantee our success. According to many *Gedolim* today, therefore, what we need in addition to our *hishtadlus*, is lots and lots of *tefillos*.

It is well known that the Steipler *Gaon*, *Harav* Yaakov Kanievsky, *Zatsal*, for example, advised parents to constantly daven for their children. And on numerous occasions, the *Rosh Hayeshiva* of Yeshivah Torah Vodath, *Harav* Avrohom Pam, *Ztz"l*, publicly attributed all of his successes in learning to the tears his mother, *A"H*, used to shed while *benching licht* on Friday nights as she davened for him to become a *talmid chacham*.

Of course, we all want the best for our children. And we all hope and pray that they grow up to be *erllicher Yidden*, productive and emotionally well balanced. What, then, can we do to increase the chances that our *tefillos* will not only be heard but will be fulfilled, as well?

The answer may be that we must daven with the proper *kavannah*. Let me explain.

The *Gemara* relates a disturbing conundrum (*Rosh Hashanah* 18a). Two people, in the exact same situation, desperately needed a *yeshuah.* "One was saved. And the other was not saved." How can this disparity be explained? The *Gemara* states that, "one davened a complete *tefillah* and was answered while the other did not daven a complete *tefillah* and [therefore] was not answered."

The obvious question here is what is considered, "a complete *tefillah?*" Rashi comments with one word, that the one who was saved davened, "with *kavannah.*" That he davened with *kavannah*?! Who could possibly not daven with *kavannah* if he was in a dreadful state?

Harav Matisyahu Salomon, *Shlita,* the Lakewood *Mashgiach,* once elucidated this enigmatic commentary of Rashi during a public address. What *kavannah* was Rashi referring to, asked the *Mashgiach.* Certainly, he could not have meant simply paying attention to his davening. Anyone in dire straits certainly pays attention to his davening. After all, what else does he have to hold onto?

What Rashi was referring to, explained the *Mashgiach,* was the specific *kavannah* that *tefillah* can really help, that it has the power to bring about salvation for everyone, even people like us. All too often, the *Mashgiach* lamented, we daven by rote, without the heartfelt conviction that *tefillah* can really bring about a significant change in our circumstances.

We want to do whatever we can to make our *tefillos* more effective. And we all want to increase the chances that our *tefillos* for our children will be answered like those of Rav Pam's mother. In order to achieve those goals, therefore, we have to daven with the *kavannah* that our *tefillos* really can help us to become all we can be as parents.

May the *tefillos* of Jewish parents everywhere for their precious *kinderlach,* both young and more mature, be answered together with the *tefillos* of all of *Klal Yisroel* for the advent of *Mashiach Tzidkeinu, bim'heirah b'yameinu, Amein.*

About the Author

Dr. Meir Wikler is a psychotherapist and family counselor in full-time private practice in Brooklyn, New York. He also writes the popular weekly column, "Partners in Parenting," in the daily HAMODIA.

In addition to over seventy articles in lay and professional journals, Dr. Wikler is the author of:

- ✓ The First Seven Days: A Practical Guide to the Traditional Observance of Shiva for Mourners, Their Families and Friends (United Hebrew Community, 1987),
- ✓ Bayis Ne'eman b'Yisrael: Practical Steps to Success in Marriage (Feldheim Publishers, 1988),
- ✓ AiSHeL: Stories of Contemporary Jewish Hospitality (Feldheim, 1994),
- ✓ Einei HaShem: Contemporary Stories of Divine Providence in Eretz Yisrael (Feldheim Publishers, 1997),
- ✓ Partners With Hashem: Effective Guidelines for Successful Parenting (ArtScroll, 2000), and
- ✓ Zorei'a Tzedakos: Contemporary Stories of Divine Providence (Feldheim, 2003).
- ✓ Ten Minutes a Day to a Better Marriage: Getting Your Spouse to Understand You (Artscroll, 2003)
- ✓ Partners With Hashem II: More Effective Guidelines for Successful Parenting (ArtScroll, 2006)

Dr. Wikler has lectured extensively to both lay and professional audiences on mental health and family life in the Orthodox community. And his clinical work has been featured in several newspapers, including THE NEW YORK TIMES and THE JERUSALEM POST.

This volume is part of
THE ARTSCROLL SERIES®
an ongoing project of
translations, commentaries and expositions on
Scripture, Mishnah, Talmud, Midrash, Halachah,
liturgy, history, the classic Rabbinic writings,
biographies and thought.

For a brochure of current publications
visit your local Hebrew bookseller
or contact the publisher:

Mesorah Publications, ltd

4401 Second Avenue
Brooklyn, New York 11232
(718) 921-9000
www.artscroll.com